The Puritans

A Captivating Guide to the English Protestants Who Grew Discontent in the Church of England and Established the Massachusetts Bay Colony on the East Coast of America

Free Bonus from Captivating History (Available for a Limited time)

Hi History Lovers!

Now you have a chance to join our exclusive history list so you can get your first history ebook for free as well as discounts and a potential to get more history books for free! Simply visit the link below to join.

Captivatinghistory.com/ebook

Also, make sure to follow us on Facebook, Twitter and Youtube by searching for Captivating History.

Contents

Introduction: A Puritanical Recipe

The Puritans. The very name invokes images of the religiously strict and austere. Those puritanical purists who considered all other religions null and void in comparison to their own. The very word "puritanical," in fact, is derived from this group of religious zealots. And zealot here is not being used in the pejorative sense but rather as a very apt description of the manner in which the Puritans lived their lives.

The Puritans believed very strongly in their religious sensibilities, and they were willing to do just about anything to see them be carried out. As was often the case with new religious movements, the title of "Puritan" was not one that the Puritans themselves came up with. It was a nickname given to them by opponents of the religious movement who ridiculed them as being unrealistic purists. Those labeled with this title took it to heart, and they took up the challenge that it meant, declaring that they were indeed Puritans, just as their adversaries had charged.

In the beginning, the Puritans were simply religious reformers who sought to separate English Protestants from the last vestiges of Roman Catholic tradition. England entered the Reformation a little bit later than continental Europe, and the initial cause of the English Reformation was much different. Initially, it was due to a falling out between King Henry VIII and the pope, which led the British king to separate from the mother church and declare himself the head of a brand-new church, the Church of England. In many ways, the Church of England was Catholic in all but name. Many of the same doctrines and rituals of the Catholic Church carried over into the Church of England. Perhaps the biggest difference was that the pope in Rome no longer had any authority over the British.

At any rate, this act opened up the floodgates, and a religious reformation began to take hold in Britain. The Puritans were against the Catholic Church and sought to "purify" their pews of any and all Catholic teachings. As they progressed as a Protestant faith, the Puritans became even more puritanical, and soon, they rejected just about all other Protestant faiths that differed from their own teachings.

But as much as the Puritans were lambasted as being hypocritical by their opponents, they did indeed try to practice what they preached. They firmly believed that if they openly lived what they deemed to be a righteous life, they could persuade others by their very example. Through their own self-sacrifice, they wished to serve as a living testament of what Christian believers should be like. But as was often the case in the aftermath of the Reformation, this interpretation of what Christians should be like was almost always a recipe for strife and conflict. The Puritans sincerely believed that it was their duty to be that "shining city on a hill" that would set the example for others. They attempted to live a life that was set apart, almost as if it would be a testimony to the world that one could follow in the goodness of God. Their intentions were good, but as often is the case with even the best-laid plans of both mice and men, such things are often easier said than done.

Chapter 1 – Before the Puritans

"That man is truly humble who neither claims any personal merit in the sight of God, nor proudly despises brethren, or aims at being thought superior to them, but reckons it enough that he is one of the members of Christ, and desires nothing more than that the head alone should be exalted."

-John Calvin

In order to really understand the religious movement known as the Puritans, you really need to understand what went on before the Puritans came about. The Puritans, of course, were successors of the Protestant Reformation that shook the Catholic Church to its core. The Reformation was sparked by a Catholic monk named Martin Luther, who began questioning official church teachings. It was Luther who, on October 31ˢᵗ, 1517, nailed his *Ninety-five Theses* to the doors of an abbey called All Saints' Church.

Luther ignited a dialogue that led to new thought among Christians, and soon, new denominations began to spring up. Prior to the Reformation, the Catholic Church, whose very name, "Catholic," is the Latin derivative of a Greek word meaning "universal," had positioned itself as the one true universal church in the land. After the

Reformation, however, there were several denominations in Europe that competed with each other to gain faithful converts.

Martin Luther, of course, became a primary leader of the Reformation, but he was not the only one. Close on the heels of Martin Luther's rise to prominence was a man named John Calvin. John Calvin is crucial to the history of the Puritans, as it was upon his subsequent doctrine of Calvinism that many Puritan beliefs and thoughts would be based.

John Calvin was a French reformer who, after being driven out of his native France, set up shop in nearby Switzerland, where he preached his beliefs on predestination. Calvin, just like Luther before him, stressed the need for faith in order for Christians to achieve salvation. Just like Luther, he believed that salvation was not something someone could earn through good works; rather, it was something one could only achieve through faith in God.

But—and this is a big but—Calvin proclaimed that God had already preordained who would be open to having faith in him and who would not. Basically, he believed that the story of life had already been written long ago, and the author of creation—God—had already created all of the parts that we would incredibly end up playing. Imagining God to be the ultimate producer/screenwriter/director of reality, Calvinists would tell you that we're all simply playing out the role we have been given. That everything that we do has been predestined and preordained.

John Calvin preached that whether we come to have faith in God or go astray and turn our backs on grace and faith, all of it had already been predetermined in advance. This viewpoint would become an important fixture in the life of the Puritans. The concept of predetermination is still a hot-button issue among Christians even today. Many Christians view such concepts as absolute anathema, feeling as though it negates the central Christian tenet of free will. Most Christians would agree that man has free will and chooses whether to do good or bad. The Calvinist idea that some are doomed to darkness while others are destined to go toward the light seems to contradict the very notion that we have free will. Then again, even Christians aghast at the Calvin doctrine of predestination would be hard-pressed to explain how a God, whom they will readily admit is omnipotent and all-knowing, would not know what our futures have in store. If God knows everything and can see the past, present, and future all at once, as most Christians would tell you, then how could He not know what our ultimate outcome would be? Some Christians, however, might contend that it's not so much that God predestined or preordained our choices but that it's just His nature to know how everything is going to play out. This wouldn't be so much predestination as rather just knowing everything in advance. Predestination, of course, is a very complicated theological concept, and it can be analyzed, viewed, and argued from a wide variety of angles, as one can see.

John Calvin's notion of "the elect," or the idea that it was a chosen few whom God had chosen to be saved, also resonated with the Puritans, who would truly come to believe that they were a people set apart. One of the great Puritan leaders of the 1600s, John Winthrop, would liken the Puritan movement to being a "shining city on a hill" for all the world to see. Winthrop did not invent this phrase; these words were gleaned from the New Testament of the Bible itself. The verse can be found in Matthew 5:14, in which Jesus declared to his followers, "You are the light of the world. A city set on a hill cannot be hidden." The Puritans would take these words to heart, and they would take it to mean that they were indeed the elect that God had set apart to fulfill his divine will.

Another Calvinist doctrine that would come to greatly influence the Puritans was the notion that all church members should be equal and that there should be no centralized authority figure to rule over them. The Catholic Church, of course, was (and still is) a highly organized and hierarchical body, in which the pope is on top with cardinals and other high-ranking members branching out below. John Calvin wanted nothing to do with any of this. The Puritans agreed, and when their movement eventually kicked off in England, they were steadfastly against the Church of England's hierarchical archbishops and bishops. The Puritans declared that they did not want these religious authorities telling them what to do.

Another tenet of Calvinism that the Puritans wholeheartedly embraced was the notion of the separation of church and state. John Calvin declared that the state government had no right to interfere or dictate matters of the church. The Puritans passionately agreed on this matter as well, and they ultimately brought this concept to America. It was in the New World that the Puritans would leave one of their most lasting legacies, as the separation of church and state would eventually become a hallmark of the later United States.

John Calvin first arrived in Switzerland in 1536, and by the 1540s, many of his ideas had firmly taken root in the region. The English, in the meantime, had been fairly inoculated from the Reformation that was sweeping the European mainland. Prevented from having such expressions of thought by stern Catholic rulers, the most anyone could do was to sit back and watch what was occurring across the English Channel and wait. Since 1509, England had been in the grip of King Henry VIII, who began his career as a staunch Catholic. In his advocacy for the Catholic Church, he initially set himself up as an opponent of the Reformation and even wrote a treatise in defense of Catholicism called the *Defence of the Seven Sacraments*. King Henry didn't have very many kind things to say about Martin Luther either; at one point, he likened Luther to a snake whose words were like "viper's venom." The pope over in Rome wholeheartedly approved of Henry's thoughts and actions, and at one point, he even proclaimed King Henry to be a "defender of the faith."

But this great defender of the faith would prove somewhat fickle and would only support the pope when he was allowed to get his way. And as it pertains to England, the break with the Roman Catholic Church came not over religious disagreements but rather because

King Henry was upset with the pope for not fulfilling his request to have his marriage annulled. Divorce was out of the question in those days, so the next best thing was to get an annulment, as it would declare the marriage to have been null and void in the first place.

Henry had been married to Catherine of Aragon for over two decades, and he was quite distressed that she had not been able to produce a male heir to the throne. Henry, feeling that his very legacy was at stake, decided he needed a new wife. Since England was Catholic, this meant that this supposedly sovereign king had to first consult with the pope. And when the pope refused to fulfill his wishes, an infuriated King Henry broke with the pope and the Catholic Church outright. However, Henry was still very much Catholic in his beliefs. He did not want to get rid of Catholic tradition; he just wanted to get rid of papal authority. It's for this reason that he created his own state-run church, the Church of England, of which he would be the head. The pope would no longer be in charge of religion for the English; now, it would fall upon their own king's shoulders to dictate to them the correct modes of religious worship and thought.

Although King Henry VIII took over England's church, he left most of the Catholic traditions and trappings intact, and it was these vestiges of the old Catholic Church that progressive-minded reformers within the Church of England sought to do away with. In a sense, they wanted to "purify" the Church of England of all former links to Roman Catholicism. It was from this mindset that the concept of Puritanism came forth.

Before the Puritans, England's pseudo-Reformation had been deemed by many to be woefully incomplete. How could any self-respecting Protestant and Calvinist believer (as many English Protestants were) tolerate the donning of Catholic-styled priestly vestments and readings from a book of prayer that harkened back to the mother church in Rome? For many, these holdovers of Catholicism were intolerable. It was as if the door to religious freedom had been cracked open ever so slightly, but no one was allowed to open it the rest of the way.

Britain's Protestants longed to have the religious freedoms that had been won by their Protestant brethren in strongholds such as Switzerland and Germany. Some fervently prayed and waited for that day to come; others, however, were willing to couple their prayers with action.

Chapter 2: The First Puritans

"It is God's will through His wonderful grace, that the prayers of His saints should be one of the great principal means of carrying on the designs of Christ's kingdom in the world. When God has something very great to accomplish for His church, it is His will that there should precede it the extraordinary prayers of His people; as is manifest by Ezekiel 36:37. And it is revealed that, when God is about to accomplish great things for His church, He will begin by remarkably pouring out the spirt of grace and supplication."

-Jonathan Edwards

Those who ended up being the founders of Puritanism did not have the intention of starting a new religious movement but of simply purifying the Protestant Church of England of all latent vestiges of the Catholic Church. King Henry VIII broke from the Catholic Church in 1534, and although his actions led to reform, King Henry VIII was not himself a reformer. Ironically enough, he began his career as a staunch supporter of the Catholic Church, which was perhaps why he kept so many of the traditions of the Catholic Church intact in his new state religion, the Church of England.

Even though the king had split with the Roman Catholic Church for temporal rather than spiritual reasons, Protestants were grateful. However, they were not excited about the continued presence of the Catholic Church in the country. Later English Protestants would work to slowly reform these aspects of the Church of England from the inside out. One of these early English reformers was Thomas Cranmer, an archbishop of the Church of England.

Cranmer championed the cause of the Church of England adopting the Protestant belief in "justification by faith" rather than "justification by works." It was perceived by the Protestants of this time that the Catholic Church was too focused on doing good works rather than simply having faith in God. Protestants knew that both good deeds and faith were important, but they wished to stress the belief that it was only through faith in God that one could gain salvation.

Archbishop Cranmer and his supporters also refused to recognize the Catholic belief in "transubstantiation," which held that Jesus was literally transformed into bread and wine during communion. Even today, it's still a strange concept for Catholics to have to explain. Transubstantiation teaches that while Christ is not in any way perceived by the physical senses during the rite of communion, a transformation does indeed take place. Although the bread and wine still look and taste just like bread and wine, the substance of the sacraments transforms into a non-physical manner during that brief moment of taking the Eucharist. Yes, even once explained, it's a hard concept for some to fathom.

Cranmer and his Protestant allies were quick to discard this often confusing and hard-to-grasp aspect of the Catholic faith. But even though King Henry VIII had broken with the Catholic Church, the king was slow to accept many Protestant beliefs. Furthermore, there was a growing conservative wing in the Church of England who did not wish to lose the old teachings of the mother church. These conditions made the English Reformation a much slower process than the rapid reform that had taken place in other countries on the European continent.

In England, political reversals often led to religious reversals, and much of the gains that the English Protestants had made could be quickly overruled. After King Henry VIII passed in 1547, power was given to his then nine-year-old son, Edward. Although he was certainly not old enough to lead on his own, Protestants were assured that his eventual reign would be friendly to their faith.

However, King Edward VI unexpectedly perished in 1553, and with him, much of the Protestant cause perished as well. For it was after his demise that Edward's sister, Mary, who was a staunch Catholic, came to the throne. Yes, ironically enough, despite all of King Henry VIII's efforts to produce a male heir to succeed him, it was ultimately his eldest daughter Mary who would come to hold real power over England.

Mary I, who would go on to develop the nickname of "Bloody Mary," would put on a full reversal of all Protestant reforms. Suddenly, it was a crime to engage in religious practice outside of Catholicism. Before Mary took her place on the throne, allegiance to the pope and Roman Catholicism was considered anathema, but once she took power, the Catholic rites were once again in fashion. Cranmer himself fell victim to this sudden reversal, and he was subsequently burned at the stake for holding fast to the reforms that had once been deemed acceptable.

However, in England, what was acceptable as it pertains to religion had almost become anyone's guess, as the shaky sands of British religious doctrine continued to shift under everyone's feet. Queen Mary I angered Britain's Protestants even further when she married the Catholic stalwart Philip, the king of Spain, in 1554. Close on the heels of this marriage was the announcement that Catholicism in England would be officially restored. Then, in 1555, Mary went a step further by putting Catholic laws regarding heresy back in place. It was this renewed push against heresy that would cost Protestant reformers, such as Cranmer, their lives.

Many more reformers, realizing that England would no longer tolerate their beliefs, made the decision to flee to Switzerland. At this point in time, Switzerland—the land of Calvinism, no less—had become a refuge for many English Protestants. And soon enough, those who could be called "Puritans" were flocking to Swiss cities such as Geneva and Zurich in droves.

Some sense of stability did not arise until Queen Mary I abruptly perished from what is thought to be cancer in 1558, allowing her half-sister, Elizabeth, to come to the throne. Queen Elizabeth I was a Protestant, and she set in motion a trend toward basic Protestant ethos that would remain in place thereafter. But whether Protestant- or Catholic-leaning, British monarchs quickly realized that they had to placate both the reformers, who sought new ways of dealing with religion, and the conservatives, who wished to maintain old traditions.

It was this ideological dichotomy of Britain that often persuaded British monarchs to take the middle of the road, so to speak. They allowed for some Protestant reform, but they also did not want to take things too far. Due to the monarchs' reluctance to fully shift the religion of the country, there were always some among the Protestants who felt that England's move toward Protestantism wasn't going far enough. This was where the Puritans came in.

Of particular early interest for those who would become Puritans was the issue of the priestly vestments used by the clergy in the Church of England. The Puritan Protestants wished to get rid of this tradition since it seemed to harken back to the Catholic Church. Instead of elaborate dresswear, Puritans recommended modest black gowns that were less flashy and ostentatious. It might seem like a minor detail today, but the dress code of the priests of the Church of England was a big deal back then.

The Puritans were downright ashamed of the slow pace of the reformation within the Church of England. This sentiment was perhaps summed up best in the anonymous tract *Admonition to the Parliament*, which was authored in 1572. The tract proclaimed its disdain, stating, "We in England are so far off from having a church rightly reformed, according to the prescript of God's word, that as yet we are not come to the outward face of the same." English-based Puritan Protestants could only look with envy at the more robust Protestant reforms taking place on the European continent.

Queen Elizabeth was indeed a middle-of-the-road reformer when it came to domestic affairs, and she was very much a stickler for keeping the status quo. But while she sought to maintain the slow pace of English reforms at home, she was quite progressive when it came to her Protestant policies abroad. Queen Elizabeth became a kind of Protestant crusader when it came to taking on Catholic Spain. It is rather ironic that her former brother-in-law, King Philip, would become her archnemesis, but this is essentially what the state of affairs was like in Elizabethan England.

Like master chess players, both of these leaders watched the other very carefully as they engaged in their own personal holy war, and whenever one made a move, the other was sure to attempt a move to directly counter their efforts. Most notably, Queen Elizabeth was a staunch supporter of the Protestant-leaning Netherlands, which King Philip was actively trying to bring back into the Catholic fold. King Philip, who had inherited the region from his father, Holy Roman Emperor Charles V, had been waging war with his proxies in the southern reaches of the Netherlands against the Protestant stronghold in the north. In 1580, after a long, protracted struggle between these factions, King Philip sent one of his loyal commanders, Alessandro Farnese, also known simply as the Duke of Parma, to try and put the Protestants of the northern Netherlands to rest.

The Protestants of the north, in the meantime, had formed the so-called Union of Utrecht, for they had pledged to band together to ward off any foreign invasions. They managed to hold their own after several incursions, but in the summer of 1585, the defenders appeared to be on their last legs right when the Duke of Parma was getting ready to unleash an all-out invasion of the northern Netherlands.

All seemed just about lost when British troops suddenly arrived on the scene, sent at the behest of Queen Elizabeth herself. As the British soldiers stepped foot in the Netherlands, the queen was signing into law an official pledge to aid the Protestants. This aid was the Treaty of Nonsuch, which declared that the queen wouldn't hesitate to use military force to defend her Protestant allies in the Netherlands. These two daring moves were enough to convince the Spanish Crown to back off, and the northern Netherlands were left in peace.

The queen's actions indicate that although she was very careful to walk a tightrope between the various factions within her own country, when it came to the larger international showdown between Catholics and Protestants, she was more than ready to go on the offensive. At home, though, she was always careful not to antagonize her own citizenry and potentially spark a rebellion by giving too much to the reformers.

On the international stage, this strong stance against Catholicism actually prompted Spain to try and invade England in 1588. But despite all of Spain's power, the Spanish Armada was successfully beaten back by the British navy. Many Protestants and Puritans alike viewed this success as a sign of divine providence at work. They truly believed that God was on their side.

At any rate, Queen Elizabeth I certainly seemed to be adept at stifling the spread of Catholic power. Even in the Americas, Queen Elizabeth was ready to take on the Spanish at every turn. Although England had yet to create a viable colony at this point, the queen was sure to employ privateers, which is basically just a fancy word for pirates, to roam the high seas near Spanish possessions in the Caribbean and beyond. These private sailors were tough as nails, and they were more than willing to seize Spanish treasure ships and haul the silver, gold, and jewels they acquired from them back to England.

Overall, as it pertains to Protestants far and wide, Elizabeth wasn't a bad ruler to have. After Elizabeth's passing in 1603, the more Puritan-minded faithful became somewhat hopeful in regard to her successor, James Stuart. James Stuart was a champion of the Protestant sect known as the Presbyterians. The Presbyterians hailed from Scotland, and prior to James Stuart being crowned in England, he was the king of Scotland, known as James VI (he became James I after the union of England and Scotland in 1603). As such, he was obviously quite familiar with these Protestants. And upon his arrival to the English throne, the idea that James I would be helpful in the Protestant cause quickly took hold.

Soon enough, Puritan Protestants put together an official petition to get the king to consider their reforms. These efforts resulted in the so-called Hampton Court Conference. King James I proved to be uninterested in most of their notions, although he did agree on one important point—there should be a new English translation of the Bible.

The Puritans were key in getting the king to set in motion the great translation project that would result in the King James Version of the Bible. This was welcomed with open arms by the Puritans, who had been calling for an English version of the Bible for all to be able to freely read for many years. The Puritans, however, did not have the favor of the king when it came to their battle against priestly vestments, and many puritanical Protestants ended up getting booted out of the church simply for declining to wear them.

Some of those belonging to the Puritan wing of the Church of England were influential enough that local clergy secretly made certain compromises just to keep them on board. But such things could not go on forever, and like oil and water, the Puritans in the Church of

England soon found themselves separating entirely and creating their very own religious movement. The most assertive of these puritanical faithful began to hold secret meetings in their own homes. These meetings were considered illegal at the time, and the fact that these Puritans did not attend the officially sanctioned Church of England was considered a crime in itself. All it took for one to be prosecuted was for a nosy neighbor or former church member to report their absence, and they would be subjected to punishment. Some even lost their lives, as was the case with reformer Henry Barrow, who was executed in 1593.

Nevertheless, despite the push to conform to the Church of England, King James was a Calvinist, and he supported Calvinist teachings. This support was clearly demonstrated in 1618 when the leading Calvinists of the day held a conference in the Netherlands. The main purpose of the meeting was to discuss the work of one Jacob Arminius. Jacob Arminius hailed from Utrecht, the same part of the Netherlands in which the Protestants of the northern Netherlands had banded together and forged the Union of Utrecht in the face of Catholic aggression. The reason why Jacob Arminius became a matter of debate was over his view that the choices of human beings could shape their destiny and that they did indeed play an active role as it pertained to whether or not they were saved. These views, although perhaps quite commonplace in other Christian groups, absolutely rubbed Calvinists the wrong way. John Calvin's teachings on predestination were quite clear, and Calvinists were to believe that God was the author and finisher of the human story, with men and women being completely unable to change the course of their destiny on their own. Nevertheless, this "reformed Calvinist," as it were, managed to gain a substantial following with his modified teachings of Calvinism, and his unique point of view was dubbed Arminianism.

Yes, once again, there was yet another variation of Christian thought springing forth. And no sooner than it did, critics and detractors came out of the woodwork. Jacob Arminius himself passed away in 1609, but in the ensuing years, his teachings continued to catch on. In order to tackle the so-called Arminianism controversy that had been emerging in Protestant circles, the great minds of Calvinism came together in the Netherlands in 1618.

King James I was sure to send his own representatives to the conference to argue for the complete rejection of Arminianism. Such efforts were most certainly pleasing to those of a Puritan bent. Even though they were not happy with the remnants of Catholic tradition in the Church of England, the knowledge that the overall Calvinist doctrine was being embraced would most certainly have been encouraging.

These positive developments were enough to keep the more vocal voices of the Puritans down, and many were content just to engage in what they called "practical divinity." These efforts focused on teaching the average person Puritan ideals by example without actually going so far as to openly disobey the Church of England.

In that same fateful year of 1618, however, some Puritans felt it expedient to circumvent the will of their king when King James I decided not to back his own son-in-law, Frederick, the king of Bohemia, in his struggle against Catholic forces during the Thirty Years' War. Some Puritans began to raise and send funds of their own accord to this potential Protestant potentate.

However, besides some clandestine efforts such as these, most Puritans were willing to tolerate King James as long as he, in turn, tolerated the main tenets of Calvinism. This mutual toleration of sorts would last for much of King James I's reign. It was at times an uneasy alliance, but it seemed to serve its purpose.

King James positioned himself as the steward of Calvinism, and he stressed that the clergy should be careful not to confuse the laity with the complexity of the doctrine. In 1622, he even went so far as to issue a command that only those who held "a Bachelor of Divinity or higher" would be permitted to teach on predestination in order to safeguard the public from further confusion.

Perhaps King James, who had witnessed plenty of upheaval over various interpretations of predestination, meant well enough, but this directive struck many as an intolerable overreach. Protestants were growing concerned that their religious rights were beginning to be taken away. Without the ability to speak freely and have an open dialogue, what would this mean for spiritual growth? The Puritans, for one, were not going to allow any sovereign to handcuff their faith.

When King James allowed his son Charles to wed a French Catholic princess, many Puritans sensed further trouble lay ahead. And when Charles I came to the throne in 1625 and began practicing Catholicism openly, they felt that their worst fears had been confirmed. It was the arrival of King Charles, in fact, that led many Puritans to seek somewhere farther afield to plant their faith—as far afield as the other side of the Atlantic, to a little-known place called America.

Chapter 3 – How the Puritans Came to America

"For we must consider that we shall be as a city upon a hill. The eyes of all people are upon us. So that if we shall deal falsely with our God in this work we have undertaken, and so cause Him to withdraw His present help from us, we shall be made a story and a by-word throughout the world."

-John Winthrop

Most Americans know the story of the Pilgrims who came to America on a ship called the *Mayflower* and how they made their home in Plymouth in 1620. But many are unaware of just how much religious piety drove these settlers to leave their old world for a completely new one. It wasn't in search of gold or land that the Puritan Pilgrims embarked on this dangerous voyage. Their quest was for religious freedom and the chance to build a society marked by the ideals that they held dear.

Plymouth Colony was only the second successful English colony in America, coming after the previous settlement of Jamestown in what is now the state of Virginia. The wooded backdrop of Plymouth would end up being famously commemorated in America on the Thanksgiving holiday, in remembrance of a time when puritanical

Pilgrims and their Native American allies sat down during the fall harvest to have a meal together and give thanks to God.

Although we now know Plymouth to be a city in Massachusetts, it was initially a part of the general colony of New England before separating off into the Massachusetts Bay Colony. The Puritans who settled Plymouth were led by a man named William Bradford. Before even stepping foot on land, the Puritans famously signed the Mayflower Compact, in which they dictated how both the colony and their own individual lives should be run. This document would prove pivotal in the shaping of America itself. It was cited by philosopher John Locke, who made his famed "social contract," which then later influenced the very creation of the Declaration of Independence that gave birth to the United States of America itself. So, to say that the words of the Mayflower Compact were influential would be a bit of an understatement.

Upon landing, the Puritans got to work building up their settlements and putting their principles to practice. Further waves of Puritan migration were in the works in Britain, and by 1630, a Puritan leader named John Winthrop was leading the so-called "Great Migration" of a large Puritan flock to the Massachusetts Bay Colony. It was named as such because of the fact that the colonization enterprise was funded by a group of London-based financiers called the Massachusetts Bay Company.

The amount of money that the Massachusetts Bay Company put on the table for this expedition is said to have totaled what would have been forty million dollars in today's money. The ships that carried these passengers to the New World were fully stocked with everything they could ever need. They were loaded with "soap, candles, tools, utensils, steel, iron, clothing, shoes, house furnishings, sail cloth, cattle, horses, goats, hay for fodder, prayer books and Bibles."

This must have come as some comfort for folks who had to sell their homes and many other belongings to even embark on this trip to a strange new world. This was indeed a major enterprise for anyone to take. As such, the man leading the trip did not want to disappoint. John Winthrop was a middle-aged attorney, an occasional preacher, and a general Protestant crusader. Winthrop was alarmed both at the pressures that puritanical Protestants were facing at home, as well as the inroads Catholicism had been making abroad.

Catholic Spain had claimed much of the Americas long ago, taking over Mexico and Central and South America. This was certainly nothing new. But Winthrop was further alarmed to hear reports of French Catholics thriving in the North American colony of Quebec. Upon his arrival in June of 1630, Winthrop went about the difficult task of creating solidarity among the Puritan settlers, many of whom had come from different backgrounds and different regions of Britain.

Settling in the town of Salem, Winthrop told his colonial congregants that they had not only entered into a covenant with one another but also "with God." Furthermore, it was taught that the New England colony would be a "city upon a hill," one that would inspire those who saw it to imitate it. Winthrop's words were inspired from the biblical Book of Matthew, in which Christ himself told his disciples, "You are the light of the world. A city on a hilltop that cannot be hidden."

Winthrop and his Puritan followers had to forge their world from scratch, building homes and eking out an existence in an uncertain world. But despite making sure that their basic earthly needs were being met, they also had the major challenge of making sure that their spiritual beliefs remained intact as well as they created a "godly kingdom" here on Earth. Over the next few years, these colonists would forge a system of governance in which they would vote for a governor and a mock parliament, which consisted of both an upper and a lower chamber of legislators.

The local houses of worship, in the meantime, were arranged in a similar democratic process, in which church leaders were selected by members of the church. The Puritan colonies, like much of the rest of the world at the time, were ultimately a patriarch society, so when we say "members of the church," we must make it clear that it was only male members who were allowed to have a say in these affairs. And the men of the church were able to not only cast votes for church leaders but also various representatives who would make up what was known as the General Court. It was the General Court that would fashion general laws in regard to how the colony was run and how various affairs of the settlers were handled.

And in order to foster solidarity among the various churches, regular clerical conferences were held in which all of the church leaders could consult with one another about the direction of the general Puritan movement. The main leaders to arise during this time were Thomas Hooker, Roger Williams, and John Cotton. At times, these men disagreed with each other, but they were always able to do so in a fairly civil manner. But even while the Puritan congregations sought solidarity, they did not always conform to the same standard. There would almost always be a slight difference in opinion on certain matters of faith.

In the meantime, many British puritanical faithful began to view their brethren across the Atlantic with some concern and skepticism, wondering if perhaps this sect of Puritanism was drifting toward a new denomination altogether. Nevertheless, the colonial Puritans maintained that they had not changed their aim. Puritan leader John Winthrop made it clear that his intention was for settlers to enter into a covenant with one another and remain strong in the alien world that they now called their home.

As much as John Winthrop encouraged open discourse to prevent conflict, disputes would inevitably arise. Roger Williams, for example, famously caused a ruckus over oath-taking and whether or not colonial leaders had the right to regulate one's activities during the

Sabbath. This Puritan was so perturbed over what was going on that he ended up moving to the nearby settlement of Providence (the future capital of Rhode Island) instead.

And the disputes didn't end there. Puritan minister Thomas Shepard had quite a bone to pick with the Protestant reformer Anne Hutchinson. Anne lived in Puritan-controlled Boston with her husband William and their fifteen children. In between taking care of all of her kids, Anne had proven to be quite a preacher. However, not all Puritans agreed with what she had to say, and Thomas Shepard, for one, was most certainly not a fan.

Shephard disapproved of Anne Hutchinson's contention that one could have a direct "spiritual connection with God." Such talked smacked of antinomianism, and Thomas Shepard and other like-minded Puritans believed that such thoughts were in error. They believed that God only directly spoke to biblical figures of the past and that his direct manifestation no longer occurred. For sticklers like Thomas Shepard, those who claimed to have a personal relationship with God were deluded at best or engaged in outright witchcraft at worst.

Those familiar with the Salem witch trials, which we will discuss in more detail shortly, realize just how quickly puritanical accusations of witchcraft can spin out of control, so such characterizations were indeed quite serious. Although most Christians today would view a personal relationship with God as being a good thing, for some of Anne's Puritan contemporaries, even one who claimed a connection to God could be accused of practicing witchcraft. And if they weren't outright calling Anne a witch, they were at the very least suggesting that she was delusional.

Anne and her followers, however, insisted that the Puritans who dismissed the spiritual connection one could have with God were the ones who were deluded. Anne believed that these particular Puritans were blinded by their emphasis on "the role of works." It's ironic that Anne would accuse her brethren of such a flaw since it was in large part due to the Catholic Church's supposed emphasis on works that the Protestant Reformation began in the first place.

Thomas Shepard and his ilk, however, felt that Anne Hutchinson seriously erred by putting too much on the "notion of free grace." Anne, on the other hand, accused her opponents of putting too much emphasis on good works and deeds rather than developing a real relationship with God. Interestingly enough, the only Puritan minister that Anne didn't accuse of being too focused on works was John Cotton, who had previously been her and her husband's personal pastor.

It seems that Anne first began to speak out on her views while working as a midwife. She and the women she regularly worked with would routinely discuss their ideas on religion, and Anne greatly encouraged these thought-provoking talks. John Winthrop would later recall of Anne "that her ordinary talk was about the things of the Kingdom of God." Having said that, most today would quite naturally ask, "Well, what's wrong with that?"

But the problem wasn't that she was talking about God but rather the subject matter she chose. At any rate, Anne was soon having regular gatherings at her house, in which she elaborated further on her beliefs and interpretation of the scripture. Initially, the attendees were mostly midwives like herself, but soon, many more began to hear of her teachings. And ultimately, both men and women regularly packed her house to hear her preach.

The two sides of this debate were increasingly at each other's throats while those caught ideologically in between, such as the more centrist John Winthrop, tried their best to find some sort of middle ground. It proved to be an impossible task. And as soon as Thomas Shepard and his hardliners gained the upper hand, they saw to it that Anne received an official excommunication and was booted right on out of the colony.

Anne, like Roger Williams before her, headed to Providence, along with her family, and created outposts in what would one day become Rhode Island. Unfortunately, Anne's life did not end very well. After staying for a time in Providence, she set up shop in the settlement of Eastchester, near the site of modern-day New York. It was here that she and her whole family met foul play at the hands of a local Native American tribe.

At any rate, internal divisions such as what occurred with Anne Hutchinson did indeed surface among the Puritans from time to time. Although the Puritans had fled from religious persecution, they were hesitant to show much in the way of tolerance when religious differences of opinion arose.

Along with these internal conflicts, the Puritan-based colonies also dealt with external conflicts as well. They faced pressures from both the Dutch, who controlled the colony of New Netherland (now New York), and several groups of Native Americans. For the Puritans settled along the Connecticut River, things became so bad that open conflict erupted with a tribe of Native Americans called the Pequot in the year 1636.

The war was basically the culmination of tensions that had been building in the region over trade, scarcity of resources, and various skirmishes that had broken out. The Puritans managed to get other local Native American tribes to side with them against the Pequot. Despite their advantage in numbers and knowledge of the terrain, the war ended up going badly for the Pequot, and once the fighting had ceased, their power was greatly diminished.

Despite the conflict, that same year, the first steps were made to establish a Puritan-backed school of learning, which would ultimately become Harvard University. The school itself was modeled after the prestigious English institution of higher learning Cambridge University. In fact, the very settlement in which Harvard was built was dubbed "Cambridge" in honor of that fact. The school originally had a heavy focus on creating ministers for the faith, but it also put a spotlight on general academia as well. At any rate, anyone who attended Harvard in Cambridge, Massachusetts, has the Puritans of the Massachusetts Bay Colony to thank for it.

The Puritans certainly had their difficulties in the colonies. But even more pressing for the American Puritans was the threat of the English Crown. At this time, the archbishop of Canterbury, one William Laud, had become practically hellbent on scaling back Puritan immigration to America. He had even openly sought to have the Massachusetts charter rescinded. The Puritans, in the meantime, feared that they would have a royal governor, who would be completely indifferent to their concerns, foisted upon them. This threat seemed to disappear when the British government became far too distracted by its own inner turmoil to bother with the Puritan colonists. For it was around this time that England would become drawn into a series of bloody civil wars. King Charles I had developed an increasingly antagonistic relationship with the British Parliament. Members of Parliament had long been skeptical about King Charles's motives, and the general public resented the fact that he was married to a woman with a Catholic background, Queen Henrietta Maria of France.

Things came to a head when King Charles attempted to throw some of his parliamentary opponents in prison. The keyword here is "attempt" since the king failed to seize his enemies. Instead, they were tipped off as to what was happening and made a break for it. It was on the heels of their escape and after the rest of Parliament learned what had happened that England turned into a country of basically two armed camps—those willing to fight for Parliament and those willing to fight for King Charles. These two sides began to face off against each other in 1642.

As the conflict heated up, King Charles I had firm control of northern England, Wales, the Midlands, and the West Country. Parliament, on the other hand, had control of London, the surrounding southeastern portion of the country, and East Anglia.

They also had a trump card at their disposal, as they had the backing of the English navy. After several skirmishes, the war was essentially a stalemate by 1644. In an effort to come to a diplomatic solution, King Charles managed to hold a new session of Parliament where he was stationed in Oxford.

The results were not satisfactory, however, and the fighting continued. Oxford was then laid siege to by parliamentary forces in 1646, and the king himself just barely managed to escape. He fled to the north, where he was hidden by loyal Scots for several months. Parliament eventually managed to convince the Scots to hand him over. King Charles I was then made prisoner in January of 1647. Because religious questions played as much of a role as political ones during this conflict, many have dubbed the English Civil War as the "War of Religion."

And as it pertains to the Puritans, many leading English Puritans did indeed side with the parliamentarians against the Catholic-influenced king, whom they held in low regard. As such, some have even gone so far as to term the conflict as being a "Puritan Revolution" of sorts, in which zealous Puritans commandeered the power of Parliament to purify England of its most obvious signs of Catholic influence—the king himself.

During the course of the conflict, Puritans also made sure that they had new legislation brought to Parliament, calling for a further reformation of the English church. The Puritans of England themselves remained splintered as to the best course to follow in regard to reforms, though. One faction of English Puritans was convinced that they should emulate the popular reforms that had been carried out by Presbyterian clergy, while others were advocates of so-called "Congregationalism," which imitated that old Puritan shining city on a hill—New England.

In the meantime, all of those in Parliament were gravely concerned should any one of these factions gain dominance, lest they come to lord it over the rest. This had commonly been the case throughout the course of all reformation movements in the past. As soon as one Protestant strain became prominent, it wasn't long before they began to persecute the rest. Time and time again, the previously persecuted religious minority rose up to become the number one persecutor.

Parliament was worried about a sudden repeat of history due to a lack of "central control" when it came to matters of faith. Many today are not aware of this learned trauma of England and other European nations during the Reformation, but it was most certainly on the minds of America's later founders. It is for this reason that the concept of the freedom of religion was so important to them, as well as the concept of the separation of church and state. Many today interpret the separation of church and state to mean keeping religion out of government, but the main focus was actually to keep the state out of religion. The Founding Fathers did not want to repeat the problems caused by the Church of England, and they did not want to establish a "Church of America" that would dictate what religious rules everyone should follow. It was therefore deemed that the best approach for society was to have a complete separation of church and state, preventing the government from dictating how churches should conduct themselves.

In the aftermath of King Charles I's house arrest, a radicalized element of the king's opposition called the Levelers began to demand the "freedom of religion" for England. But before these plans could come to fruition, in 1648, King Charles escaped from his confines and managed to independently reach out to the Scotts, and he convinced them to side with him once more. This led to the so-called Second English Civil War, which erupted between the king and Parliament. This time around, the king was even less successful and was rather quickly defeated. He was then captured for a second time.

Not taking any chances, his opponents put him on trial and subsequently sentenced him to death. King Charles I's death sentence was carried out in January of 1649. This then led to Parliament attempting to forge a commonwealth, but the fickleness of the parliamentarians led to one too many disagreements, and the whole thing threatened to come undone. Stepping into this chaos was Oliver Cromwell, who seized power in 1653 and created the Protectorate of England.

Styling himself as the Lord Protector of England, Cromwell was essentially little more than a dictator. Cromwell was also a Puritan. Oliver Cromwell first came to prominence during the First English Civil War and had become a leading military commander by the time of the second one. Cromwell was pivotal when it came to reining in the Scotts and allowing for King Charles to be taken into custody. And since Cromwell was himself a Puritan, he considered it imperative to purify England of the vestiges of Catholicism. He saw himself as God's own tool in this enterprise, and he firmly believed that he was put in place uniquely for that very purpose.

Cromwell is sometimes referred to as a "reluctant" dictator. He was not an elected official and had merely seized power after the king had been deposed. Cromwell himself often spoke that he didn't want to rule England and that his reign was a reluctant one forged out of necessity.

Interestingly enough, Cromwell still remains a polarizing figure among the British public, with some likening him to an evil usurper and others insisting that he was more akin to a guardian figure. And just as his title implied, he was indeed a "Lord Protector" of the realm. At any rate, once he had power, he didn't hesitate to use it as it pertained to religious affairs.

Cromwell was also at the forefront of what had become a kind of Protestant crusade against the Catholic power of Spain. It was under Cromwell that Jamaica was seized from Spain and brought into the British fold. At home, meanwhile, Cromwell was an important

Protestant reformer who sought out the help of Congregationalists and the more centrist among the Presbyterians in order to find some common ground.

In 1646, Cromwell issued the Westminster Confession of Faith, which dictated that the particular brand of Calvinist doctrine that was so pleasing to both Presbyterians and Puritans alike became the religious law of the land. Also, Puritans were politically rewarded with an increasing number of seats in Parliament.

As one might imagine, the fact that the Puritans were being treated so favorably did not sit well with those who were opposed to Puritan ideals. These opponents may have been temporarily sidelined by the new reforms, but they were just biding their time and waiting for the right time to strike. And upon Cromwell's sudden and abrupt death in 1658, yet another religious reckoning would arrive.

Chapter 4 – Puritan Paradise Lost

"In all your course, walk with God and follow Christ as a little, poor, helpless child, taking hold of Christ's hand, keeping your eye on the mark of the wounds on his hands and side, whence came the blood that cleanses you from sin and hiding your nakedness under the skirt of the white shining robe of his righteousness."

-Jonathan Edwards

After the death of Oliver Cromwell, a struggle for the control of England ensued that ultimately ended up inviting the son of Charles I, Charles II, to come to the throne in the year 1660. Interestingly, it was not the new king but rather Parliament that began to move against the English Puritans. The Church of England regained much of its authority, and the Puritans were relegated to the fringes as dissenters who refused to conform. Even as Puritans were facing renewed persecution in England, back in the British colonies in America, the opposite was the case.

The Puritans who ran the roost in the colonies were becoming increasingly intolerant to other faiths. Most notably, when the Quakers began to emigrate to America in the 1650s, the Puritans, who were often their neighbors, began to persecute them for their religious beliefs.

One of the most famous of these cases occurred when a Quaker woman by the name of Mary Dyer was given a death sentence simply for speaking to others about her faith. Despite the risks, Mary had frequently preached to others about Quaker beliefs in the Puritan enclave of Boston. She was arrested and ultimately led to the gallows as punishment for her unsanctioned evangelizing. Before her death, she was told that if she would simply swear an oath that she would desist from preaching her Quaker beliefs, she would be spared. One must wonder if this was a particularly cruel trick on the part of her Puritan prosecutors since they knew full well that as part of their faith, Quakers refused to swear oaths.

Predictably enough, Mary Dyer refused as well, and she was subsequently hanged. Many were disturbed by what had happened to Dyer, and by the time the story reached England, King Charles II was moved enough to do something about it. In 1661, he launched an official edict to all who resided in Massachusetts Bay to cease and desist with any executions of Quakers on the specific orders of the king. In addition to this, a royal commission was dispatched to the colonies to check on colonial authorities and make sure that they were not overstepping their bounds.

Among other things, this commission made sure that the Puritans were not excluding other religious denominations from communion. This pressure to be more accepting of other religious denominations, along with the economic boom of the colonies, opened up the doors for religious settlers of all kinds to make their way to the colonial settlements in New England. This new influx led to social conflicts in many of the colonial communities. Although outright persecution of other faiths had been banned, resentment continued to simmer just underneath the surface.

Nevertheless, there would be external threats that would bring further tension to the colonists. This was the case in 1675 when Native American tribes launched large-scale attacks in the New England area in what was later termed King Philip's War. It was named after one of the main agitators, Chief Metacomet, sometimes known simply as Metacom, who had been given the nickname of King Philip.

Metacom had apparently come to the conclusion that the European settlers had simply become too numerous, and he rightfully recognized that the growing number of settlers was becoming a threat to his tribe's very existence. Despite previously friendly relations, Metacom essentially launched what could be considered a preemptive strike against the burgeoning Puritan population.

During the course of this conflict, local tribes launched several raids against the colonists, as well as the tribes with whom they had remained allied. During the course of these raids, some six hundred colonists would lose their lives, and several settlements would be destroyed. It is said, in fact, that during the conflict, which would last until 1678, at least twelve settlements were completely annihilated, and a whopping 10 percent of the total population of the colony was wiped out.

The Puritans, falling back on their beliefs during this difficult time, of course, came to consider their problems were somehow related to their faith. Many developed the firm conviction that what had happened to them was somehow a direct punishment from God. It is not hard to understand why the Puritans and other Protestants might consider a disaster such as this as being some sort of divine retribution. All they had to do was look at the Old Testament and read through the testimonies of biblical prophets who, at different times in the nation of Israel's existence, claimed that it was God's punishment being unleashed upon them when neighboring tribes attacked.

Just like the Israelites were ready to ascribe blame for hardship, the Puritans too began to openly wonder if they had committed some collective sin for which they were being punished. One of the Puritan preachers who championed this view, Increase Mather, was a native-born Puritan of the Massachusetts Bay Colony. Having "Increase" as a first name might seem a little strange to the modern reader, but there was indeed a reason behind it. His parents had been quite steeped in scripture at the time of his birth, and knowing that the Hebrew form of Joseph, *Yosef*, translated into English literally means "Increase," they decided to name their child Increase in honor of that fact. Naming kids either Yosef or the anglicized version of Joseph is common, but actually naming them the English translation of the original Hebrew is indeed a rarity in modern times. Among the Puritans, however, such things were commonplace.

At any rate, Increase Mather, whose parents arrived with that great exodus from England to the Massachusetts Bay Colony in 1630, was among the first generation of Puritans to be born in a New England settlement. He grew up during the good times of the early settlement, during which Puritan Pilgrims and Native Americans lived in relative harmony. This was then juxtaposed with the horrific experience of King Philip's War and the terror it brought about.

In the aftermath, Increase Mather was one of the Puritan leaders who did not hesitate to put forth the claim that they were suffering due to a lack of spiritual renewal. Increase Mather, whose name literally signifies an increase of blessing, sought to renew and increase the spiritual blessings of the Puritan Protestants. Increase believed that God sent various judgments upon the people in order to get them back on track, and he considered the recent hardships as a sign that the Puritans of America needed to change course.

The colonies of New England were indeed vulnerable, but it wasn't the local tribes that the colonists feared the most but rather the English government back home. After Cromwell's death, many of the gains the Puritans had made in England were rolled back under King Charles II, and when Charles II was succeeded by King James II in 1685, this new king applied even more pressure. This time, the king's efforts were directed on the New England Puritans themselves, for it was King James II who decided to completely revoke the Massachusetts Bay charter altogether. King James II then opted to establish the Dominion of New England in which all of the established colonies, along with New Jersey and New York, were combined into one overarching dominion of the Crown. This meant that there would be a royal-appointed governor general to oversee everything and that there would no longer be any democratically elected legislative bodies put in place to represent the colonists.

Even worse, and much to the chagrin of the Puritans, was the forced introduction of the hated *Book of Common Prayer*. The *Book of Common Prayer* was the official standard liturgy of the Church of England at the time, and once it was put in force, everyone was expected to adhere to it. This was most definitely not the direction that the Puritan colonists wanted to be going in. And what galled them the most was the fact that their own town meetings—the lifeblood of the Congregationalists—had been curtailed, strictly controlled, and monitored.

It was indeed particularly distressing to the Puritans that even in the New World, which they had immigrated to in order to freely practice their religious beliefs, they were not immune to the long reach of a determined enough English king. And as if all this wasn't enough, King James II was himself a practicing Catholic, which only fueled suspicions that Protestant Puritans were going to be suppressed to the point of ceasing to be a distinct body within the Church of England.

But as paranoid as the New England Puritans might have been in contemplating the machinations of their sovereign, the Puritans in

England were ready to overthrow King James II outright. The incident that managed to send James II's opposition over the edge was the news that his wife had given birth to a son named James Francis Edward. Normally, the birth of a royal heir would have been a joyous occasion. But the idea of a James III on the throne, who would potentially continue on the same course as his father, was not something that was looked forward to, especially since it had been previously stated that James II would transfer power to his Protestant daughter, Mary, thereby making her Protestant husband, William of Orange, the king. It was this promise that had made things at least somewhat tolerable to the Protestants of England, and most were content to wait for that day to arrive. But when it was learned that Mary was going to be pushed out of the way in favor of a child who would be raised in the Catholic faith, it was too much for the opposition to tolerate.

Fed up with the way things were going, Parliament actually contacted William of Orange (Orange is a region in southern France) behind King James II's back and invited him to come to England and remove King James II by force. William of Orange leaped at the invitation, arriving on British shores with fourteen thousand troops at his disposal. This was enough to frighten King James into abdicating, and he sought refuge in France. William of Orange was then made the new king of England, christened King William III in 1689.

That same year, back in the New England colonies, a major revolt in Boston, known as the "Bloodless Revolution," managed to break the iron grip of New England's dominion status. In later years, Boston would become the centerpiece of many protests of English governance, culminating in the infamous Boston Tea Party of 1773. At this point in time, though, the king may have been a bit too distracted due to the fact that fighting had erupted between the British and the French in what is now the Canadian provinces of Nova Scotia and Quebec.

King William III, who came to the throne with way too much on his plate, was not willing to duke it out with the colonists as well. Instead, he readily agreed in 1691 to allow the New England settlements to break back into their various distinct identities, with the sole exception of Plymouth, which was absorbed into Massachusetts.

But although the Puritans had regained some influence, they did not have the political power that they previously did. It was still a time of great uncertainty in regard to what direction the colonies would go. New arrivals, who came with new ideas on both religion and civic life alike, were threatening to change the way things had been done.

In other words, the Puritan monopoly of New England was at an end. And it was during this time of high anxiety that a court packed with Puritan agitators in Salem, Massachusetts, would begin the most sensational court proceedings in history, known simply as the Salem witch trials.

Chapter 5 – The Witch Trials in Salem

"Let them no more say, God must do all, we can do nothing, and so encourage themselves to live in a careless neglect of God, and of their own souls, and salvation. Most certainly, although we cannot say, that if men improve their natural abilities as they ought to do, that grace will infallibly follow, yet there will not one sinner, in all the reprobate world, stand forth at the day of judgment, and say, Lord, thou knowest I did all that possibly I could do, for the obtaining grace, and for all that, thou didst withhold it from me."

-Increase Mather

If someone today were to accuse you of being a witch, you might give them a strange look and perhaps even let out a nervous laugh, but in 1692, in Salem, Massachusetts, such things were no laughing matter at all. Witches were not some cardboard cutouts from some Halloween make-believe world; for the Puritans, witches and the concept of witchcraft were quite real. They looked to none other than the biblical accounts of witchery, such as when Israel's King Saul consulted the Witch of Endor, to verify that witches were indeed a force that they had to contend with.

In the Old Testament, there is a clear account of witchcraft that takes place when a very troubled King Saul seeks to summon the spirit of the dead prophet Samuel. Previously, Samuel had been King Saul's guiding light, but after his passing, King Saul fell on hard times and sought advice. Although God had forbidden the practice of the occult, Saul, in his desperation for answers, secretly met with a witch who—according to the Bible—was indeed successful in summoning the spirit of Saul.

The prophet was none too happy that his rest was disturbed, and he chastised Saul for using the arcane arts to find answers to his problems. This biblical account indicates that sorcery and witchcraft are indeed real; it's just that God has forbidden human beings from engaging in any of it. The Bible strongly cautions against humans meddling with forces that might be too powerful to fully understand.

Having said that, the Puritans would have used the Bible as a reference when considering the possibility of a real-life witch in their midst in Salem. The Puritans believed the scriptures, and since the scriptures indicate that witches are real and, in some instances, could even summon spirits of the dead, the Puritans, therefore, believed this was real as well. And since the scriptures clearly condemn the practice of these dark arts, the Puritans likewise condemned anyone who they suspected of witchcraft.

And in the remote, rugged world in which they lived, late at night as the wind blew through the trees and animals could be heard scurrying about, it wasn't hard to imagine that witches might be on the loose. The Puritans believed in the forces of good and evil. They believed that some were influenced by evil, but others had good on their side. Of course, such beliefs were entirely dependent on the other person's perspective. The Puritan preacher Samuel Parris, for one, thought that he was on the side of good.

Parris had founded a Puritan church in Salem Village in 1689. It's important to note the distinction between what was then known as Salem Village and Salem Town. Both areas are part of Salem, but they represent two very different sections of the settlement. Salem Town was situated on the eastern shores of Salem proper, and it had a bustling port where all manner of goods were traded back and forth across the Atlantic. Due to the commercial success of Salem Town, many of Salem's more affluent individuals began to pour into this district.

The section of Salem known as Salem Village, however, was much more backward, with ramshackle housing. After a period of decline, it became known as a haven for the poorer classes. Life in Salem Village was much harder than it was for those who lived near the harbor in Salem Town. Most of the residents of Salem Village were farmers, and when their farms failed to produce enough revenue for them to get by, they often turned to religion for answers. Was there a divine judgment at work to explain these crop failures? It wouldn't have been at all unusual for someone in Salem Village to think such thoughts.

The church founded by Samuel Parris would have been the main focal point for most of the Salem villagers. They turned to their pastor for guidance during times of hardship and difficulty, and they also looked to him for moral guidance and how they should conduct themselves.

After being installed as the new arbiter of morality in Salem Village, Samuel Parris rapidly developed a reputation of being a strict and stern disciplinarian. Some were resentful of this fact, especially some of the newcomers to Salem Village, but Parris stood firm. And for some, rather than being repelled by his preaching, they were drawn to them. These were hard, uncertain times. New England was still recovering from the rampant depredations of King Philip's War, along with the recent ravages of King James II's war with the French, coupled with the ever-changing order of how the colonies were administrated. The Puritans still had influence, but they were no longer the sole authority.

It was in the midst of all of this uncertainty that people began to literally look for signs of the devil at work. And when Samuel Parris took to the pulpit and claimed that the devil was "in their homes," that the devil was in "their farms," and even "in their church," they believed him! Parris himself would then become the center of the evil that he so often spoke of when his nine-year-old daughter Betty and his eleven-year-old niece Abigail Williams appeared to be afflicted by an unseen force. They screamed, fell to the ground, writhed, and rolled across the floor, claiming that some unseen entity was biting, scratching, and hitting them. The whole village was on high alert for such happenings, especially after Cotton Mather—the son of Increase Mather—published his famous book *Memorable Providences*, which discussed in depth supposed signs of witchcraft.

In the centuries since these young girls erupted into these spells and fits, many have tried to figure out just what might have brought it all on. The most common explanation offered today is that the girls were simply faking their affliction to get attention. These girls lived a lonely life of drudgery. Brought up in the hard frontier country of America, their days consisted of a long list of chores and manual labor around the house and surrounding property. The best they could hope for in life was to marry well, as a man with means might be able to ease their burdens in their later years. These girls got up early, worked hard, said their prayers, and went to bed early before starting their routine all over again. Perhaps they were craving a break from the monotony and desired to be the center of attention. It's not too hard to understand why they may have felt this way; it's just mind-boggling that they would go to such extreme lengths to get it.

Nevertheless, if the whole thing really was a ploy to get attention, the girls were most likely caught up in their own game and unable to admit the truth lest they become severely punished for their deception. It very well could be that the whole thing simply spiraled out of control, and once the mischief had begun, no one—not even the ones behind it—were able to stop it.

Frantically trying to get answers from the young girls as to what was the matter, Parris learned from them that they had been engaging in superstitious activities with his servant, an old Native American woman by the name of Tituba. They claimed that Tituba had engaged in acts of divination, such as dropping an egg in a glass of water and then interpreting what the congealing egg yolk might mean. Such things probably sound silly to us today, but back then, it was a big deal. And when Reverend Parris learned that two other girls in Salem—Ann Putnam Jr. and Betty Hubbard—were displaying similar afflictions, folks began to think that the whole town was suddenly under siege by dark forces. Ann and Betty were then soon followed by another pair of girls, Mary Walcott and Mercy Lewis, who also came forward with the same exact symptoms.

The fact that so many girls came forward makes the idea that they were just lying for attention a little harder to entertain. It's not to say that the girls didn't fake it—they most certainly could have. It could very well be that they all had the same friend groups and had quietly confided in one another as to what they planned to do. The Putnam family, for one, was quite close to Reverend Parris and his family, so it wouldn't be hard to imagine these girls all getting together to discuss what they were going to do.

But nevertheless, the more bewitched girls you add to the mix, the harder it is to say with certainty that every single one of them was simply putting on a show for the villagers. With so many girls behaving in this fashion, it goes from just a couple of girls deceiving their elders to a much more elaborate plot of several girls working in tandem. Again, this very well could be the case, but it certainly complicates matters.

Then again, there are other explanations that have been offered. Because while some believe that the girls were making it all up just to get attention or even as a means to lash out at villagers they didn't like, others have theorized that perhaps they suffered from mental illness or even a common affliction brought on by some sort of food poisoning that caused them all to hallucinate. And although it's probably the least popular premise in modern times, there are those who still might consider that perhaps some supernatural force really was afoot.

At any rate, as the "bewitched" girls continued to speak to town leaders, the list of people they accused continued to grow. And by February of 1692, they had three women in their sights. Along with Tituba, they also accused a lady named Sarah Good, who was essentially a down-and-out beggar who depended on the kindness of her neighbors for meals and a roof over her head. Another woman that they claimed was a witch was Sarah Osborne, a woman who tended to stay home from church—something that was frowned upon by the villagers.

The common thread between all three of these women was that they were all on the fringes of Puritan society. The servant Tituba, due to her background and status as a servant, was an obvious outsider to the Puritans. Sarah Good was someone who didn't work and went from home to home. She was an object of scorn among her peers. She initially came from an affluent family, but after her dad—a well-to-do innkeeper—committed suicide some twenty years prior, Sarah Good fell on hard times and never quite recovered.

Sarah Osborne had a complicated and what many of her neighbors viewed as a "scandalous" past. At one time, she was a prominent member of the community, and she and her husband, Robert Prince, owned some 150 acres of farmland. After her husband died, Sarah shocked her neighbors by taking out some fifteen pounds (British money) to "buy" an indentured Irish servant by the name of Alexander.

Many today are not aware of the practice, but indentured servitude in those days was quite common. It was expensive to travel from Britain to America, so some who did not have the immediate means to pay for their trip agreed to sign a contract that would make them an indentured servant for so many years in order to pay for their trip across the ocean. Alexander had apparently agreed to just such a bargain, and he planned to work for Sarah Osborne in a state of indentured servitude until his debt was paid off. If this wasn't enough to get the Salem villagers talking, what she did once he paid his dues really got their tongues wagging. To their shock, she actually married the young man. This caused the neighborhood gossips to run wild for a variety of reasons, but most importantly, they focused on the perception that Sarah must have been intimately involved with her indentured servant before she married him. Just imagine Sarah Osborne at the local market or seated in a church pew with gossipy locals behind her, whispering of what they believed to be scandal of the highest magnitude. Just put yourself in Sarah Osborne's shoes, having to sit back and listen to people say things like, "Oh did you hear about what Sarah Osborne did? She bought a man for fifteen pounds and then married him!"

Yes, one can only imagine how difficult it became for Sarah, having to deal with this constant stream of gossip. It was so difficult, in fact, that she stopped attending church and going to many other social gatherings. But as is always the case, the more she isolated herself, the more people talked about her. This caused people to openly speculate and wonder what she did with her time. Quite frankly, the villagers simply thought she was weird. And the town gossips perhaps had already openly commented that she was a witch as it was, so it probably didn't come as much of a surprise when the "bewitched" girls proclaimed this to be the case.

At any rate, the following month, all three of these accused women were hauled off to jail so that they could be interrogated. Isolated and alone before their accusers, they were all asked the same repetitive questions, such as "Are you a witch?" "Have you seen the devil?" "What did the devil tell you?" and the like.

No matter how many times one protested that they were not a witch and did not speak to Satan, the interrogators persisted, trying to get them to crack under pressure. As for one of the women—Tituba—it wasn't hard at all to get her to admit that she was a witch. Tituba, in fact, soon openly admitted engaging in all manner of witchcraft and magic. It is important to remember that due to Tituba's religious background, which included ancestral shamanism, some of her ancestral religious beliefs would indeed equate to witchcraft in the eyes of the Puritans. And even if she did not engage in some of the things she claimed, it seems that Tituba was clever enough to realize that the more she told her interrogators, the happier they were, so she readily obliged them. And her accounts were quite incredible to hear.

She said that a tall, dark figure would visit her in the middle of the night. She claimed that he would also shapeshift into a "great black dog." This demonic entity apparently began hassling Tituba to "sign his book" and pressured her to serve him. This interaction seems to borrow from a mixture of both Christian and ancestral lore. Many Native American tribes believe in beings who are shapeshifters. The Navajo tradition of "skin-walkers," for example, is one of the more famous manifestations of this belief.

Thrown into the mix with this shapeshifting entity, at least according to Tituba's account, was a kind of evil counterfeit of the Christian Book of Life. Christians believe that all who are saved have their name written in the Book of Life. This demonic entity, however, supposedly wanted Tituba to sign her name not into the Book of Life but in a book reserved for death and the damned. A book that she said she signed with her own blood.

The most troubling thing about Tituba's testimony is the fact that she readily implicated the other accused women. If she was making things up to save herself, it would be one thing, but she also began to openly claim that Sarah Good and Sarah Osborne were her accomplices. She stated that she and the other two women had all rode through the air on wooden "poles." In other words, she claimed that she and the other women rode on broomsticks in true, classic witch fashion. Tituba went on the record to state, "I ride upon a stick or pole and Good and Osborne behind me. We ride taking hold of one another. I don't know how we go for I saw no trees nor path, but was presently there."

And fantastical as all of these claims were, it wasn't hard for the Puritans, steeped in their religious beliefs, to consider that these tales were true. All of these women were on the fringes of society, and claims of them delving into the dark arts were not too surprising to the superstitious-minded Puritans. To believe that a poor beggar, a shunned outcast, and an indigenous woman were witches wouldn't have been much of a stretch for them at all.

But on March 11th, 1692, when the bewitched young girls began to accuse Martha Corey, a well-respected Puritan woman, of being a witch, the situation became downright scary for the villagers of Salem. If Martha could be a witch, then anyone could be a witch. Now, many were beginning to take the words of the Puritan preacher Samuel Parris quite seriously, for it seemed that evil truly was lurking around every corner.

The interesting thing about Martha Corey is that she was one of the few townspeople to voice her concerns that perhaps the girls were making things up. She had openly wondered if the young women's claims were more the product of make-believe than real supernatural happenings. It was shortly after she expressed her doubts of the girls' claims that they turned their ire upon her and began to accuse her of also being a witch. This has led some to wonder if perhaps the girls made up stories about Martha Corey as a means of revenge for her lack of belief.

Upon being accused, Maratha Corey stood firm and famously declared, "I never had to do with witchcraft since I was born." However, it didn't matter how many times she denied being a witch; she was declared to be one regardless, and she ended up losing her life as a result of this false (at least most would consider it false) charge against her. In the end, despite all of her cries of being innocent of the charges leveled against her, Martha Corey was hung in the town square that September for all of the Puritans to see. This sent shockwaves through the Puritan community, and many began to fear both that their neighbors might be engaging in witchcraft and that they themselves might somehow be accused of being a witch.

Many soon realized that the best way to avoid suspicion would be to seem that they were actively on the offensive against witches. Soon, pretty much the whole community was aiding Puritan leaders in hunting for witches in Salem. Yes, the witch hunt had truly begun. Both women and men were brought in for questioning about their daily routines, with interrogators probing every aspect of their lives as they looked into the possibility that these accused just might be seeking an audience with Satan.

Incredibly enough, even little kids were accused of witchcraft, and at one point, Sarah Good's four-year-old daughter was even taken in on charges of being a witch. Soon, the local jail was so crowded that there wasn't even enough food to feed all of the prisoners. As such, some actually starved to death before their case went to trial. Others died of contagious maladies that they picked up from fellow prisoners.

By May 1692, Massachusetts Governor William Phips convened a court that would try these accused witches, which was called the Court of Oyer and Terminer. This was a Latin phrase that means "to hear and decide." It is important to note that by this time, girls were no longer the only accusers of witchcraft. Friend had turned against friend and neighbor against neighbor to avoid having accusations thrown at them. Women were not the only ones accused either, as men were not spared from the witch hunt. However, women were accused more often than men.

The first to stand before this court was a woman named Bridget Bishop. Bridget, by all means, was at odds with typical Puritan life. She was a woman who seemed to often flout Puritan rules and traditions. She was a heavy drinker, played games of chance, and liked to wear clothing that defied Puritan convention. Her accusers put forth the claim that Bridget had made herself known to them in "spectral" form. The girls claimed that Bridget would send her invisible specter to them and would hit, kick, bite, and otherwise torment them. They claimed that she was doing this even while testifying in the courtroom in front of the magistrates.

The magistrates demanded to know how Bridget was appearing before the girls in spectral form and how she was afflicting such torment upon them. All manner of accusations were heaped upon Bridget. Among other things, it was also claimed that Bridget had the uncanny ability of "transforming into a cat." As mentioned earlier, the concept of shapeshifting, along with broomstick riding, had become an established facet of witchcraft lore.

Upon hearing of the charges leveled against her, Bridget, of course, was just as confused as anyone else, and she insisted that she didn't know what they were talking about. Despite her protestations of innocence, she was given the hangman's noose all the same. In fact, she was the first person to be killed during the trials, dying on the gallows in June 1692.

The interesting thing about how the Puritans conducted the Salem witch trials is the fact that it encouraged false confessions. Those who openly confessed to being witches were often spared, whereas those who steadfastly proclaimed their innocence were often killed. Ironically, it was the very Puritan principles of honesty that led many innocent men and women to their graves. Those with less integrity readily lied about being witches and even about others being witches if it meant that their own life would be spared.

The truly honest and devout Puritans, in the meantime, would not falsely claim to be a witch even if their life—quite literally—depended on it. Bridget Bishop, for one, claimed her innocence up to her last breath, proclaiming, "I have done no witchcraft. I am as innocent as the child unborn." Yet, as much as we today tend to sympathize with these victims of the Salem witch trials, it is important to note that their prosecutors often believed just as firmly in their cause, no matter how deluded we today might think it may have been. This is evidenced by a letter sent from Cotton Mather to his uncle, John Cotton Jr., which seemed to extoll the virtue of what was happening at the time. As the witch trials heated up, Cotton Mather wrote, "Our good God is working of miracles. Five witches were lately executed. Immediately upon this, our God miraculously sent in five Andover witches." Miracles indeed.

Chapter 6 – The Salem Witch Trials Continue and a Puritan Witch Hunt Ensues

"It is absurd to think that anything in us could have the least influence upon our election. Some say that God did foresee that such persons would believe, and therefore did choose them; so they would make the business of salvation to depend upon something in us. Whereas God does not choose us for faith, but to faith. 'He hath chosen us, that we should be holy' (Ephesians 1:4). Not because we would be holy, but that we might be holy. We are elected to boldness, not for it."

-Thomas Watson

As the Salem witch trials progressed, it soon became clear that literally no one was safe from being accused of witchcraft. This was evidenced when a minister of the Puritan faith, George Burroughs, was accused of being a witch. And he was not only accused of being a witch but also of being a so-called "ringleader of witches." It would have been bad enough to be a witch, but to be their ringleader?

George may have had some among the Puritans who did not care for him, but he was an upstanding citizen by their own standards. This made the accusations being leveled against him all the more shocking. George Burroughs was brought in for interrogation before Puritan judges in April of 1692.

The signs of enchantment that his accusers presented were a bit bizarre, to say the least. One claimed that George had recently exhibited "inhuman feats of strength" due to the fact that he was able to lift up a musket by "inserting his finger into the barrel." He was also criticized for his failure to baptize his kids, among other things. Some also even claimed that Burroughs had the decidedly witch-like ability of flying. All folks had to do was picture Burroughs perched on top of a broom or with his finger in a musket, and they believed that he could be a witch.

In the end, George Burroughs was marched to the gallows and hung on August 19th, 1692. Just prior to his killing, he was heard reciting the Lord's Prayer. The fact that he did so successfully was important, as the witch hunters claimed that someone who was a witch would be unable to do so. Some in the crowd were dismayed by this and openly wondered if perhaps Burroughs was innocent after all. Firebrand Puritan preacher Cotton Mather was on the scene, however, and he was quick to remind everyone that Burroughs had been, in his words, "convicted in a court of law."

The Salem witch trials serve as a reminder that a "court of law" heavily skewed by public opinion and mob-like instincts is not always a court of justice. In at least one case, when an accused woman by the name of Rebecca Nurse was found to be not guilty, the judge actually overruled the jury and declared that she was guilty. Rebecca had been accused by a powerful Puritan family who held a grudge against her, and apparently, their word was deemed to be better than hers. Or, for that matter, even the word of some thirty-nine people who put their names on a petition, demanding her release. The petition contained a statement, which read, "We never had any cause or grounds to suspect her [Rebecca Nurse] of any such thing as she is now accused." Nevertheless, she, too, was executed.

The fact that the presiding Judge, William Stoughton, intervened tells us a few things. It shows us that this trial by jury was not fair in the least, but it also indicates that those in charge knew that if Rebecca Nurse was found not guilty, it would serve to delegitimize many other cases. This was due to the fact that the bewitched girls had carried on with their antics, claiming that Nurse was spectrally attacking them just as they did with all of the others. If the girls who accused Nurse were somehow wrong, mistaken, or worse—flat-out lying—what did that mean for all the other people they had so dramatically accused prior to Nurse?

Those in charge knew that if Rebeca Nurse was let off the hook, it would spread doubt as to whether or not others had been wrongly accused. They knew that this would create a domino effect of doubt, and they did not know how they would be able to handle it. Obviously, they realized what they were doing was not right, but they themselves were stuck in the trap just like everyone else and did not quite know how to dig their way out of it. Although Nurse would be hanged for her supposed crime, her name would be exonerated not even twenty years later.

And as it pertains to George Burroughs, Cotton Mather, sitting on his high horse, declared that even the devil himself was able to transform "into an angel of light" and that it would be prudent, therefore, not to be persuaded by an accused man's proclamations of innocence. Despite Mather's insistence, however, it was soon quite clear that a grave injustice had been committed. In fact, the government of the Province of Massachusetts Bay (the successor of the Massachusetts Bay Colony) later cleared Burroughs's name and gave Burroughs's widowed wife some fifty pounds as compensation.

Cotton Mather would never apologize for his role in all this. Mather himself was perhaps just as caught up in the hysteria of the times as everyone else. In many ways, Mather was an incredibly insecure man. He spent most of his life trying to live up to the high standard of success and respect that both his father, Increase Mather, and grandfather, the famous preacher John Cotton, had been garnered during their lifetimes.

The Mather name was indeed a well-known one in New England, and Cotton Mather had developed a bit of a complex in his quest to fill those rather sizeable shoes. He also developed a pronounced stutter. His stuttering is said to have been so bad in his youth that it prevented him from immediately joining the ministry. Instead, he was steered in the direction of becoming a medical doctor. Cotton apparently gained some control over his stuttering and made his way into the ministry just like his forebearers.

Still, many felt that he wasn't living up to the standard set by his father, and Cotton Mather would be plagued with self-doubt much of his life. As many historians have pointed out, it was this mixture of a man with something to prove and the uncertainty afoot in Salem at the time that just might have been the perfect recipe for disaster.

By the fall of 1692, the Puritan residents of Salem began to have some serious reservations about what was happening. The aforementioned Cotton Mather's own father, Increase Mather, even spoke out against the witch trials. That October, he boldly stated, "It were better that ten suspected witches should escape, than that one innocent person should be condemned [executed]."

Many began to suspect that some of the wild accusations being made were due to nothing more than petty grudges. And in some cases, they were made just to get land from those that they accused. Sarah Osborne, in particular, was targeted by Ann Putnam in part because her family desired to take some of Osborne's land. The Putnam family apparently had an outstanding dispute with Osborne over their property lines and believed that Sarah Osborne had encroached upon their land. The excuse of witchcraft then conveniently presented itself as a reason to take the old lady's land from her.

It was only when Governor Phips himself became concerned enough to personally oversee the trials that things began to change. On October 12th, 1692, Governor Phips finally intervened and put a stop to what was happening. After bringing the trials to a grinding halt, Phips insisted that there must be clear evidence of someone committing witchcraft in order for them to be prosecuted. Phips stated that hearsay evidence of one person making up claims about another would no longer be admissible in court. There would no longer be wild claims of "spectral evidence." Now, only clear, concrete proof would be admissible in the Salem witch trials. Under this new standard, it was soon obvious that just about everyone who was being held was being incarcerated without any proof of any wrongdoing whatsoever.

As such, when the trials reconvened in 1693, almost all of the prisoners of the Salem witch trials had to be released. Governor Phips then made sure that anyone still remaining behind bars on account of charges of witchcraft was officially set free by May of that year, declaring that a grave injustice had occurred in this Puritan colony. Considering the fact that at least twenty people died as a direct result of this travesty of justice, this was by no means an exaggeration.

And even those who were released and survived the tumult ended up scarred for life, both by what they had gone through and the lingering suspicion that hung over them. Although many survived the trials, it is believed around two hundred people were accused; that is two hundred people who have been released back into the community, wondering why their neighbor turned on them. It is very possible that some neighbors still thought the freed could have been witches and spent the rest of their lives looking for more evidence. As mentioned earlier, some of the families who fell victim to the Salem witch trials were later financially compensated. However, for the families that were directly affected by this puritanical purge, all the pounds in the world were likely not enough when it came to the lives of the loved ones that had been lost.

The frenzied fanaticism of the Salem witch trials seemed to showcase all of what critics had long felt was wrong with the Puritans. They wanted to be a pure, shining city on a hill set apart from others. But at least as it pertains to Salem, in their quest for self-righteous purity, instead of standing out as an example of what others should do, they stood out as an example of what a society should not do.

Even now, the Salem witch trials and, of course, witch hunts in general have become synonymous with persecution and the unfair targeting of groups and individuals. If someone today were to claim that an investigation had turned into a "witch hunt," they mean to say that it is a biased and unfair inquiry. And the meaning of that phrase comes from the Salem witch trials.

Famed playwright Arthur Miller wrote his own rendition of the Salem witch trials with his classic work *The Crucible*. The piece was written in the 1950s when the panic of the Red Scare (the fear of the rise of communism that mainly found a home in the United States) was at its height. The Iron Curtain had descended across Europe, and the two superpowers of the US and the Soviet Union stood on each side of the divide with world-destroying nuclear weapons aimed at one another.

Those living in the United States in the 1950s lived in very uncertain times, much like the Puritans in Salem. No one knew when the bomb might drop, and along with this external threat, there was a considerable fear of the enemy taking root within. These fears were not entirely unfounded since Russian spies were indeed uncovered in various espionage plots aimed at the United States. It was these Russian spies that became the new bogeyman.

Just like in Salem, there was suddenly a witch around every corner. In much of America in the 1950s, just about anyone and everyone could be suspected of being a communist or a communist sympathizer. And once the House of Un-America Activities Committee (a group created to hunt out communist subversives) got through with them, they could have had their reputations ruined for life.

Those who merely got their reputations ruined were actually the lucky ones since others paid with their very lives. Critics like Arthur Miller felt that the communist scare and this rush to convict suspected subversives were very similar to what had happened in Salem. The Salem witch trials had become a standard for critical-thinking individuals to point to when they felt that the horrors of history were repeating once again.

This was a definite turning point, and the Puritans of New England would never be quite the same again. It wasn't until January 14th,1697, that the Massachusetts legislature felt enough guilt to declare a day of mourning for those people of Salem who had fallen. In a kind of memorial service, townspeople fasted and prayed for both those who were victimized and those who had preyed upon their victims.

It was in the middle of this outpouring that former witch trial judge Samuel Sewall issued a public apology. Incredibly enough, the firebrand puritan preacher Samuel Parris, who had stirred up so much of this drama, showed no remorse. Many held him accountable, however, and facing pressure from disgruntled members of the flock, Parris chose to leave Salem altogether.

Still, the scarred collective of Salem needed some sort of closure. There had to be a final reckoning, a coming to terms with what had happened. And in 1702, the Puritan survivors actually submitted a formal petition to ask the colonial courts to grant them "formal restitution" so that they could clear their name. Just like those blackballed for communism in the 1950s, folks who had been labeled as a witch in the 1690s had been made into social pariahs. Even after being released, their reputation was in tatters. Survivors felt that someone needed to finally clear the air.

The most the local courts would do was to introduce a piece of legislation that expressly forbade spectral evidence. Phips had already forbidden its use during the Salem witch trials, but now, it was in official legislation for all to see that so-called spectral evidence was no evidence at all. It was hoped that this declaration would serve to retroactively vindicate those wrongly accused since the form of "evidence" that had been used against them had been rendered null and void.

Perhaps the greatest vindication came in 1706 when an older and wiser Ann Putnam admitted to falsely accusing fellow Puritan residents. As hard as it may have been for them, these wronged Puritans utilized the most important Christian principle of all—forgiveness—and were able to come to terms with Ann, despite the fact that she had so spitefully used them.

Old Tituba, who survived her own charges of witchcraft, also expressed remorse in her role of accusing the other women. In later testimony, she claimed that she was threatened and coerced by the Puritan preacher Samuel Parris. At the behest of the girls who accused Tituba of practicing witchcraft, Parris had demanded to know all about her dealings with the devil. Tituba claimed that it was the threat of physical force that caused her to give false testimony.

Even this terrible episode, when seen through the Puritan lens, was a learning experience and a matter of faith.

Chapter 7 – Puritans in a Period of Decline and a Moment of Transformation

"God is the highest good of the reasonable creature. The enjoyment of him is our proper; and is the only happiness with which our souls can be satisfied. To go to heaven, fully to enjoy God, is infinitely better than the most pleasant accommodations here. Better than fathers and mothers, husbands, wives, or children, or the company of any, or all earthly friends. These are but shadows; but the enjoyment of God is the substance. These are but scattered beams; but God is the sun. These are but streams; but God is the fountain. These are but drops, but God is the ocean."

-Jonathan Edwards

The Puritans of England proved to have a much shorter shelf life than the Puritans of the New World. The Puritans had reached their height under Oliver Cromwell, but after Cromwell's demise, they faced backlash for what was perceived as their role in not only the death of King Charles II but also the subsequent tyranny of Cromwell. After the restoration of 1660, Puritan Protestants in England were on life support as a movement. The popular will was against these Puritans like never before.

Really, it can be said that the end of the Puritans as a definitive movement in Britain can be traced back to the year 1662, for it was that year that the British Parliament ratified the so-called Act of Uniformity. This act stipulated that all churches in England must adhere to the officially sanctioned forms of prayer, worship, sacraments, and other rituals as stipulated in the *Book of Common Prayer*. After this declaration was made, well over one thousand Puritan ministers made it known that they would not follow the Act of Uniformity. All this managed to accomplish for them was their immediate removal from their churches. From here on out, all ministers had to show evidence that an officially sanctioned bishop had given them proper ordination. There was no way around it. In the immediate days after their removal, many ministers broke down and came back to England's state-run church, ready to conform.

Those who decided to continue their dissent (called Dissenters) would remain shut out of official church business for a century and a half. Not only that, but they were also shut out of the two major institutions of education—Oxford and Cambridge—as well as other branches of public education. It makes one wonder if the Puritans who remained on the fringes like this viewed themselves as being persecuted by the "Beast" from the Book of Revelation. Every century, there seem to be Christian groups that come to believe that they are being ostracized and, as the Book of Revelation says, are unable to buy or sell or do much of anything without taking the mark of the beast.

For the Puritans of the late 1600s, that "mark" may very well have come to represent the call to conform to the state's prayer book. However, as much as they were shut out of the government's discussions, the disenfranchised Dissenters received some aid when the British Whig Party moved to oppose these court religious policies and instead made the argument that the so-called Dissenters ought to be able to have their own worship services held separate from the Church of England.

These efforts ultimately led to the Toleration Act of 1689. This allowed the Dissenters, who would ultimately be called Nonconformists by the 1700s, to have churches of their own. But Puritanism as a movement in England by this time was practically nonexistent. In America, on the other hand, after the debacle of the Salem witch trials in 1692, the Puritans underwent a dramatic transformation.

During the 1690s, the Puritans were increasingly known as Congregationalists. These congregations centered around clerical associations, which were used "for fellowship and consultation." The Cambridge Association in Massachusetts was among the first, which was founded in 1690. Here, Puritan ministers met and consulted with each other right on the campus of Harvard University. It was here that they would hold debates and consult with one another over the latest developments among their congregations. By that fateful year of the Salem witch trials, 1692, two more congregations were founded, and then a fifth was created in 1705.

By the 1700s, America was in the grip of the new, more rational line of thought that was a trademark of the so-called Age of Enlightenment that was being embraced on both sides of the Atlantic. This embrace of logic led to a downturn in religious interest, which caused many Puritan leaders to long for a revival. Congregational church leader Jonathan Edwards managed to spark one with his flock in Northampton, Massachusetts, in 1735, and he later wrote of the local surge in religious zeal in his *A Faithful Narrative of the Surprising Work of God in the Conversion of Many Hundred Souls in Northampton.*

Jonathan Edwards came from a long line of hardworking men of the cloth. His great-great-grandfather was a British preacher who perished during an epidemic in London in 1625. His widowed wife eventually married a man named James Cole, who took her and her son, William, to the newly founded colonies that were sprouting up in New England. William Edwards grew up and put his roots down in Hartford, Connecticut, where his son Richard came into the world in 1647. Richard then went on to marry and have six kids, one of whom—Timothy Edwards—was born in 1669.

Timothy would go on to become a Puritan preacher in May of 1694, and he wed a woman named Esther the following fall. It was from this union that Jonathan Edwards was born on October 5th, 1703. Johnathan was closely educated by his father Timothy, who, as well as being a Puritan preacher, also ran a kind of elementary school for local children. It is from Johnathan Edwards's school papers as a youth that we get an idea of just how brilliant of a mind he had. From an early age, he was writing whole treatises on everything from the color spectrum of rainbows to the nature of the soul. His paper on the refracted light of rainbows was apparently inspired by his studies of one of the great minds of the Enlightenment, the British scientist Isaac Newton, whose groundbreaking work *Opticks* changed much of what the scientific world understood at that time. It was Edwards's academic paper on the nature of the soul, however, that showed that he could delve into matters of the spirit just as easily as matters of science.

It was on the strength of both of these twin intellectual drives that Johnathan Edwards entered into Yale in September of 1716. Edwards finished up his collegiate course with the university in the fall of 1720 before embarking upon a career in the ministry in 1722. His first gig as a minister actually came at a Presbyterian church in New York. As noted previously, the Presbyterians and the Puritans always had much in common, and the fact that this preacher of staunch Puritan stock would preach at a Presbyterian church is not at all unusual. In fact, Edwards did not see anything in the Presbyterian doctrine that went counter to his own convictions and faith as a Puritan. Again, it is important to realize that Puritanism is not exactly defined as a denomination as much as it was a movement and mindset dedicated to keeping Christian beliefs "pure" of the vestiges of Catholicism. Having said that, if one were to view Puritanism as being a denomination, it would be the Presbyterians who would have had the most in common with them. After all, Presbyterians at this time shared the same Calvinist beliefs as the Puritans. Both Puritans and Presbyterians believed in predestination and what that belief entailed, so Edwards no doubt felt he was in good company. Jonathan Edwards's stint at this Presbyterian church would be brief, however, and he would end up leaving the Presbyterian parish in April of 1723.

His next major assignment would be preaching at a church in Northampton in 1726, where he received his ordination in the spring of 1727. Edwards soon endeared himself with his flock, and through good times and bad, he managed to captivate them through his sermons. In 1733, during a particularly bad year in which the colony was plagued both by locusts in the summer and an epidemic of influenza in the fall, Edwards's keen insight managed to galvanize them like no other.

His sermons were so thought-provoking, in fact, that he was convinced to write them down and have them published. It was these rousing sermons that found their way to the printed press in 1734 under the title of *A Divine and Supernatural Light, Immediately Imparted to the Soul by the Spirit of God, Shown to Be Both a Scriptural and Rational Doctrine*. This is admittedly a wordy title, but it is one that serves to sum up Jonathan Edwards's own traditional puritanical beliefs in juxtaposition with the trend toward more rational, logical thought brought on by the Enlightenment. Here, Edwards makes the case that rational reasoning alone is not always sufficient. At one point in his dialogue, Edwards states, "Experience shows things in a different light from what our reason suggested without experience."

From all his time studying rainbows and refracted light, Edwards knew that even though when staring at a rainbow head-on, one might reasonably conclude that it was a solid structure descending from the heavens. However, experience would make one quickly realize that this is simply not the case. This is why a four-year-old just might run across a field in search of the end of a rainbow, whereas a forty-year-old would know from experience not to waste their time.

In other words, reason isn't infallible, and logic only takes us so far—it's our experience that can lead us the rest of the way. In the aftermath of the Salem witch trials, a time when superstition seemed to run amuck, many turned away from leaning on their faith. But in many ways, Edwards, with his unique approach, managed to make it okay once again to be a Christian thinker. This seemed to open up the floodgates for a much more involved flock at his church in Northampton.

But this small-scale revival in Northampton proved to be just a mere prelude to the Great Awakening to come. The religious movement known as the Great Awakening was led by an Anglican preacher by the name of George Whitfield (sometimes spelled as Whitefield). Whitfield had already been a firebrand preacher in England when he left the British shores for America in August of 1739. After arriving in America, Whitfield proceeded to tour the New England colonies in 1740. He preached for several days on end to thousands of people in multiple locations. Like a religious rock star performing for sold-out concerts, Whitfield galvanized those who came to listen to him with his passionate, often theatrical preaching of the Bible. Whitfield was not only a great orator, for he was also good in print, and he made sure that newspapers wrote about him and that his sermons were widely distributed on the printed page.

Many Puritans were drawn to Whitfield's sermons, but it must be noted that Whitfield's style and the context of his preaching often differed from most Puritan ideologies. Old-school Puritans valued modesty and a life of outward good work, one in which they set a good example (just think of the city shining on a hill), whereas Whitfield focused on inner feelings, was passionately emotive, and encouraged his listeners to express themselves on an emotional level.

As it pertains to the Puritans who accepted this new mode of religious expression, they were referred to as the "New Lights" (as in the new lights on the hill, perhaps). And the ones who wished to hang on to the old ways were called the "Old Lights." Over the next couple hundred years or so, these two ideological camps would square off against each other in consideration of what the true Puritan ideal should be.

It was in the aftermath of the Salem witch trials, when logic seemed to be lacking, and the Enlightenment, in which logic and reason became the centerpiece, was on the rise that these two poles of Puritan thought emerged. Whitfield's sermons served as an alternative to the logic and human reasoning of the Enlightenment while steering clear of unbridled fear and superstition. Whitfield's sermons often stressed the need for God's help when it came to our corrupt human nature, as well as God's fury over sin and the human need to repent.

Many Puritan leaders supported the movement, but some of the Old Lights were critical, feeling that the theatrics of Whitfield simply went too far. There was now a significant wedge between the Old Lights and the New Lights, and this division would not be rectified until 1758. It was the very year that Jonathan Edwards's *Original Sin* came out, the same year that this old Puritan standard-bearer passed on, that the Puritans began to move on as well.

Chapter 8 – The New England Puritans and Patriots

"We must delight in each other, make others conditions our own, rejoice together, mourn together, labor and suffer together, always having before our eyes our commission and community in the work, our community as members of the same body."

-John Winthrop

In many ways, the Puritans had always been on the front lines in the struggle for American independence from England. In fact, the first colonists of what was then known as New England made greater independence from the mother country a common objective. The pilgrims who arrived on the *Mayflower* entered into a social compact with each other, as they were determined to uniquely define their role and exactly how they wished to live. John Winthrop came a decade later in 1630 with many more like-minded Puritan souls and went so far as to declare that the Massachusetts Bay Colony that they were establishing was going to be nothing short of a shining city on a hill. One that not only England but the whole world could look upon with admiration and wonder.

Instead of toeing the line, the Puritans sought to forge a shining example. Many argue that these words were the beginning of what has become known as American exceptionalism, that rugged individualism that sets America apart from the rest of the world. The Puritans had all of this in mind centuries before anyone dared to officially break with England. It was the Puritans who set the standard that the Sons of Liberty and other independence-minded groups of the mid-1700s followed in their eventual struggle for independence from the British Crown.

Jonathan Edwards, in particular, voiced the need to be free from the burden that the British might had placed upon the religious concourse in America. Denominations loyal to the Church of England quite obviously had a problem when the American Revolution erupted. The Quakers also had issues since they were committed to being pacifists. The Puritan-based faith, on the other hand, had no problem at all in putting its members behind the rebellion against the British.

In fact, the Puritans had practically been in a state of rebellion with both the Church of England and the English government all along. All of the previous Puritan stands against British governance served to work as a perfect template for those who were willing to take things to the next level and break from England outright. For those of a Puritan bent, there was nothing to lose and everything to gain when it came to finally freeing that shining city on the hill from English authoritarian aggression.

And it wasn't just on an ideological level that the Puritans inspired those poised for revolution, for they also aided and abetted on a real-world level by putting many Puritan boots on the ground. But it was no doubt the Puritan boots in the church who continually prayed for God's help in beating the British oppressors that had the greatest impact on the American Revolutionary War, for it was this continued ideological presence of the Puritans that would serve to inspire continued resistance to the Crown.

Boston, of course, served as the center stage for the infamous Boston Tea Party in which American Patriots dumped English tea into the harbor in protest of excessive taxation. The city of Boston itself was founded by Puritans. The Boston Tea Party, which took place in December of 1773, was mostly attended by God-fearing men who wished to shake the bonds of what they believed to be British tyranny. There were, of course, a few among them whose motives were a little less than pure. Some no doubt enjoyed smashing open the chests just for the base thrill of vandalism, and a few even helped themselves to some expensive tea leaves, stuffing them into their trousers. But for most, it was not anarchy and brazen theft that they were after that night but rather a catalyst to inaugurate in clear and concrete change on the part of their British overlords.

The British Empire had not only been trying to tell folks how to spend their money and subjecting them to high taxes but also telling them how they should worship God. This was where Puritan-minded folks drew a line in the sand and decided to rise up against their oppressors. The Puritans knew from their own collective experience that if such transgressions went unanswered, the transgressor would simply take it as a license to transgress even more.

It was the day after the Boston Tea Party had run its course that a lawyer by the name of John Adams declared that what occurred was not a travesty. To him, it wasn't a waste dumping tea into the harbor but rather "the most magnificent movement of all time." He further stated, "There is a dignity, a majesty, a sublimity, in the last effort of the Patriots, that I greatly admire."

John Adams was a Founding Father of the United States, and he would one day go on to become a US president. He also just so happened to be from a strong Puritan background. Adams later contended that his mentality had been developed from birth, citing the fact that he was born in 1735 when the colonies of New England were gripped between two ideological poles, that of the Enlightenment and that of the Great Awakening, which largely espoused Puritan ideals.

The Great Awakening also served as a demarcation line between the Old Lights and the New Lights, of which John Adams's generation was a part. Adams made the switch to a more progressive, New Light version of Puritanism when he was just a young teenager. He had come to dislike what he saw as irrational dogmatic views of earlier Puritans and instead embraced a more liberal approach, which was led by the teachings of the New Light dynamos Lemuel Briant and Jonathan Mayhew.

It was Mayhew who perhaps had the most influence. Mayhew championed the rights of citizens to rebel against unjust laws. He made these views quite clear in 1750 when he gave his famous sermon, "Discourse Concerning Unlimited Submission and Non-Resistance to the Higher Powers." In this sermon, Mayhew insisted that it was the common citizen who should be the proper judges of government officials, not the other way around.

The concept of a nation run on democratic principles, in which the common citizen would elect representatives, would end up sticking with John Adams. He later recalled the power of this particular sermon, stating that it "was read by everybody; celebrated by friends, and abused by enemies." And Founding Father John Adams, for one, would most certainly remember it when he helped draft the Declaration of Independence in 1776, which opened with the phrase, "We the People."

The United States was built upon the principles that Puritans, such as Mayhew, espoused. It was meant to be a republic designed by the people and for the people, and it drew heavily upon these Puritan values as a result. Later historian and 19th-century writer J. W. Thornton proclaimed that it was Mayhew's Puritan-infused sermon that served as "the morning gun of the revolution." It was as if Mayhew, in his great oratory and intellectual introspection, had issued a call to arms, and the British taskmaster didn't even realize it.

But nevertheless, those keen to keep and even expand upon their liberties in America took note. Just prior to Mayhew's discourse, Puritans of the Province of Massachusetts Bay were already in an uproar with the Crown over the ability of Anglicans to have part of their taxes redirected toward the building of churches and other monuments for the Church of England. Although the Toleration Act had forced Puritans to accept other religions, these developments clearly indicated the favored status of the Church of England. In 1749, one angry Puritan fired off a pamphlet in which readers were reminded that the Anglican bulwark of King's Chapel had been literally built upon the bones of Puritans since its foundation had been carelessly laid over old Puritan burial grounds. The pamphlet decried the fact "the ashes of the dead were inhumanely disturbed, in order to build the King's Chapel." The writer then pointed out that renovations had been scheduled that very year, and it was likely that even more of the Puritan dead would most likely be disturbed in the process.

However, more pertinent for Puritan Congregationalists were the growing calls from Anglicans to have a colonial bishop appointed with a direct line to the king of England. In the wake of all of this Anglican intrigue over King's Chapel, both the Puritan dead and living were indeed disturbed—disturbed enough to help start a revolution.

Puritans and Patriots alike were inspired not to sit back and complain about their lot but to actually do something about it. Men like John Adams took what they had learned from the Puritan tradition to heart and employed these principles in the founding of the United States of America. It may have been a shining city on a hill, but it was not the possession of some foreign crown; no, the Puritans had decided long ago that it was the common man who would call the shots.

And even as the opening salvos of the first guns of the revolution began to ring out, these Puritan-minded Americans were determined to make these principles a reality. Mayhew promised in his speeches that it was indeed possible to be loyal and yet still reach for freedom. And as the Puritans and the Patriots readied for the Revolutionary War, their conscience was clear in the knowledge that they were serving a higher calling. Both Puritans and Patriots, the inheritors of that original New England Charter, were ready to fight for what they viewed to be their God-given freedoms if need be.

Chapter 9 – Puritans, the Civil War, and Opportunities for Expanded Outreach

"Be not so set upon poetry, as to be always poring on the passionate and measured pages. Let not what should be sauce, rather than food for you, engross all your application. Beware of a boundless and sickly appetite for the reading of poems which the nation now swarms withal; and let not the Circean cup intoxicate you. But especially preserve the chastity of your soul from the dangers you may incur, by a conversation with muses no better than harlots."

-Cotton Mather

By the early 1800s, the Puritans and their congregational churches were again subjected to a period of change. Many had lost their tax privileges, as was the case in 1818 for the Connecticut Congregationalists and then again in 1833 for the Massachusetts Congregationalists. At this point, many other denominations had moved onto the scene, such as Baptists, Methodists, and, of course, the ever-present Presbyterians, who had only increased in number.

Puritans of Congregationalist churches, however, didn't fit into a nice and neat category, and they often opted to simply name their houses of worship as "First Church." If one lived in Ipswich, it would therefore be the "First Church of Ipswich"; if a Puritan flock set up shop in Townsend, it would then be the "First Church of Townsend." It was a simple yet ultimately confusing logic that left the Puritan churches with such sublime monikers.

For the Puritans of this period, the most important thing was the structure of their congregational model. Just as was the case in the past, they eschewed having to answer to any centralized authority. The proto-Puritans broke from the Pope in Rome, then the first generation of Puritans broke from the bishops of the Church of England. The later Puritans of the 1800s likewise refused to have centralized "synods, conferences, or assemblies." Although the congregations were loosely affiliated through doctrine and tradition, they were authorities unto themselves and insisted on handling their own internal affairs.

From the Pilgrims all the way to the 1800s, the Puritans held fast to the notion that each church had its own founding compact, a constitution, if you will, that created a "covenant" between church members and their particular church leader. As much as churches wished to remain free of outside control, inside the church, matters were often rigidly prescribed in advance. It wasn't uncommon, for example, for a Congregationalist church to actually have assigned seating.

However, these rigid internal controls often made the Congregationalist churches seem rather unwelcoming to newcomers who had to figure out where they would be in the hierarchy. And at times, they even had to figure out where they might be able to sit! As such, the expansion of these churches proved to be slow. For a while, these Puritan churches remained mostly in the region of the former New England colonies where they had originated. Meanwhile, after the American Revolution, Methodists, Baptists, Presbyterians, and the like managed to expand to just about every corner of the newly forged United States of America.

Despite their shrinking influence, the Puritans who remained leaned heavily on their history and tradition. In the former New England region, Puritans focused on the guiding moral compass of their Puritan forefathers and their robust faith in the "divine providence" of God. They harkened back to their Pilgrim ancestors, who believed that they weren't merely travelers to a new world but God's own actors chosen to fulfill his great commission. Their trend toward Calvinism did indeed lead them toward a belief in the preordained, and they believed that in God's divine plan, He had chosen them long ago to carry out what He needed them to do. They were also convinced that history repeated itself, and they looked to the Bible to see this cyclical cycle of events at work. All they had to do was look at the biblical Book of Exodus and how the Hebrew people were launched on a pilgrimage from Egypt to Israel. As one might guess, this story struck a chord with the Puritans, for they too saw their own exodus across the Atlantic from England in a similar way.

This melding of the past and present was also often convenient fodder for Puritan "jeremiads," which shined a light on the current folly of others through parallels with those who had gone astray in scripture in the bygone past. The biblical prophet Jeremiah was where much of the jeremiads were derived since it was that particular prophet who often preached to Israel to repent or face the wrath of God. Jeremiah was known as the "weeping prophet," in fact, and prior to his eventual martyrdom, he persistently proclaimed that God's judgment was coming upon Israel.

The Puritan preacher Jonathan Edwards, who was mentioned earlier in this book, was well known for his jeremiads. In fact, he could have been said to have written a whole treatise of these comparisons and exhortations in his famous sermon, "Sinners in the Hands of an Angry God." Edwards, just like Jeremiah before him, stressed that God placed his believers in a covenant relationship with him, but if those said believers were to go astray, that covenant could be removed.

To the Puritans, the jeremiads both expressed their unique relationship with God as well as warned them that if they did not do their part, they could ultimately lose their "continued blessing." The Puritans of the 19th century were constantly worried about losing not only their blessing but also their entire way of life. Not so much from outside oppression, as their forefathers had once faced, but from just sheer complacency on the part of their own parishioners.

And Puritan leaders began to warn their flock of this. Pastor William Lunt had just such a message for his Puritan flock when he delivered a stern warning to them in 1840. Lunt reminded them of all the Puritans who had lived and died for their faith in the years gone by, dramatically referencing their graves "in yonder burying ground." He also mused on what it might be like to have these deceased saints rise from the grave and walk right through the church doors "in ghostly procession."

After imagining the dead paying the church a visit, Lunt then asked the question, "What think ye would be the lessons that would be uttered by those ministers of Christ? Would they not say to you; Preserve the institutions which we, in our day, exhorted men to honor. Desert not the sanctuary of your fathers. If you must renounce our dogmas, do not—oh do not—renounce our principles. Or fall from a life of piety and Christian righteousness." This is some pretty powerful imagery, to say the least, and it was used in an attempt to bring home the importance of keeping the traditions of their Puritan ancestors alive, lest the dead themselves were forced to come back and remind them to do so.

At this point in time, two distinct wings of the Puritan Congregationalists rose up: those who believed that a kind of Christian perfectionism could be established and those who held fast to Calvinist doctrine that stressed the inescapable pull of original sin. This would be important in the years leading up to the American Civil

War since it was those seeking this "moral perfection" that began to seriously consider the evils of slavery. They understood that neither they nor America as a whole could be morally justified until the scourge of slavery was eradicated. This determination was on full display in 1852 when a total of forty-four congregational churches met in Mansfield, Ohio, to sign a doctrinal statement against slavery.

Nevertheless, as the Civil War erupted in 1861, the Puritans stayed mostly silent. Christians, in general, found themselves torn between the opposing sides. Some Christians were quite vocal about their support of the North's quest to end slavery in the South. Quaker churches, for example, even those located within the Deep South itself, were steadfastly against the practice, and they found themselves at odds with their own fellow Southern residents.

Christians on both sides of the ideological divide tried to use scripture to justify their viewpoints. When the war came to a close in 1865, the Puritan Congregationalists sought to reorganize their congregations. In order to stave off their dwindling numbers, many embarked upon church-building programs. Part of this outreach was aimed at the Southern states that had just been defeated by the North. The South, of course, was in great turmoil and upheaval in the aftermath of the Civil War. Even in the midst of this turmoil—or perhaps even because of it—the Congregationalists sought to expand their reach.

Indeed, some Congregationalists felt that the aftermath of the Civil War would provide new opportunities for ministry, which was demonstrated in the previous year at a Congregationalist conference for the General Association of Illinois. According to writer and Puritan researcher Margaret Bendroth, this conference, which took place in April of 1864, focused on the theme of "shackles being 'struck from millions of slaves' and 'vast regions and populations' opening up to 'free thought, speech and free missions.'" In other words, they thought that the South might just be ripe for the Puritan ideals of the Northeast to take hold. After this conference concluded,

Puritan preacher Will Patton was remembered to have boasted about "the many Congregational churches that will soon dot the South, now that the gospel and the polity of freedom can have unrestricted access to those fertile regions, from which slavery has hitherto shut out Puritan influence."

They say that God works in mysterious ways, and the Puritans, for one, believed that the trauma of the Civil War would actually serve a greater good and open the door to the hearts and minds of Southerners so that they could consider Puritan ideals. After the assassination of Abraham Lincoln in 1865, however, many Puritans, just like many other Americans in general, took a harder line against the Southerners and began to rethink having any outreach with them at all.

At the Boston Council of Congregationalists, which met shortly after Lincoln's death, Puritan Alonzo Quint famously not only railed against Southerners but also the British. This ire was provoked by the fact that the British, who still viewed America largely as an enemy, had tacitly supported the Confederacy. This support was never in an official capacity, but it was quite obvious that the British wanted to make the war as hard and costly on the North as possible. Alonzo pointed this fact out right in front of a British delegation of Puritans at the conference, charging that it was the British who were "always ready to follow the powerful, and always ready to crush the weak—robbing in India [and] plundering Ireland."

Britain, which had already outlawed slavery several decades before in 1807, was most certainly not aiding the Confederates because they agreed with them but rather did so as a means of weakening and wreaking revenge against the US itself. This aid was always on an unofficial level since the British officially remained neutral during the course of the war. Nevertheless, there were Puritans, such as Alonzo, who were ready to disown the South and all those who had ever supported them, whether that support was official or unofficial. Such fiery rhetoric could more or less be ascribed to the passions of the moment. A costly war had just been concluded, and the president, who many Puritans had looked toward as a great role model, had been cut down. There were many, of course, who were deeply upset by all of these things. This fiery indignation would cool down over the next few years, though.

And by the so-called Pilgrim Jubilee of 1870, which celebrated the 250th anniversary of the arrival of their Puritan forefathers on the *Mayflower*, Congregationalists were pushing toward what they termed to be a denominational unity. Many critics, however, pointed out that the trend toward a denominational unity would lead to too many compromises, with the overall doctrine of these Puritan inheritors becoming much more liberal as a result. And after the so-called Creed of 1883 was introduced as a unifying statement of faith, many felt it gave far too much away in the name of that said unity. One Massachusetts Congregationalist by the name of William Deloss made this very argument. In 1883, when the new creed was introduced, he mused that "[even a] professed Christian man who believes that we are descended from monkeys" would be deemed acceptable under the charter.

The debate over Darwin's theory of evolution, of course, was a major hot-button issue in the late 1800s. Those who held Puritan-based traditions close to their heart often used it as a wedge to separate themselves from those who simply called themselves true believers. For an old stickler like Deloss, it would have been anathema for a so-called Christian-believing evolutionist to be allowed into the flock.

William Deloss was just one of many conservative Old Lights who were trying to slow the change of pace in the Puritan faith. With time, however, the descendants of the Puritans would indeed become much more free-thinking and liberal in scope.

Chapter 10 – Modern-Day Puritans and the End of an Age

"The gospel brings tidings, glad tidings indeed. To mourners in Zion, who want to be freed. From sin and Satan, and Mount Sinai's flame good news of salvation, through Jesus the Lamb. What sweet invitations, the gospel contains, to men heavy laden, with bondage and chains. It welcomes the weary, to come and be blessed. With ease from their burdens, I Jesus to rest. For every poor mourner, who thirsts for the Lord. A fountain is opened, in Jesus the Word. Their poor parched conscience, to cool and to wash. From guilt and pollution, from dead works and dross. A robe is provided, their shame now to hide. In which none are clothed, but Jesus' bride. Though it be costly, yet is the robe free. And all Zion's mourners, shall decked with it be."

-William Gadsby

At the dawning of the 20th century, the descendants of the Puritan faith had reached a crossroads in their religious journey. Rather than insisting that their way was the only way, Puritans began to develop a decidedly more liberal approach. Suddenly, there was a push among Congregationalists to refrain from judging the faith of others while still holding fast to their own doctrines and traditions. One of the more famous writers and researchers of Puritanism, Margaret Bendroth, pulled up a quote from a Puritan Congregationalist, dated 1925, that seems to sum up this sentiment well. In her book, *The Last Puritans*, she documents the words of a Puritan descendant who had gone on the record to state, "We are ready to let the other fellow have his belief [but we] refuse to give up the faith of our fathers." Outsiders also seemed to soften their views of the Puritans a little bit, and the 300th anniversary of the Pilgrims landing in Plymouth was rang in with great fanfare all across the United States in 1920.

The summer of Massachusetts in 1920 was especially filled with parades, pomp, and circumstance. At one point, a parade boasted over one hundred costumed figures, which then participated in a massive and elaborate reenactment. Puritan Congregationalists in the years between the two world wars also developed a stance that has been likened to being somewhere "between blind patriotism and blind pacifism."

Unlike the Quakers, who were often conscientious objectors, the Puritans never sought to keep their youth from going off to war, but at the same time, they taught them to think very carefully as to why they were doing so. The Congregationalists had indeed maintained that fierce independent-minded spirit, and realizing they only owed their allegiance to their creator, they encouraged their members to be critical thinkers who could decide for themselves whether or not the wars their earthly government fought were worth fighting for or not.

It was in between the two world wars that an activist arm of the Congregationalists emerged, known as the Council for Social Action (CSA). This group took it upon itself to address the social issues of the day, such as fascism, racism, and economic difficulties. By the 1930s, of course, there were a lot of these social ills to take on, considering the rise of the Nazi Party in Germany, fascism in Italy, racial tensions at home, and the aftermath of the Great Depression.

This heavy focus on social issues, especially the idea of leveling the playing field as far as the economy was concerned, may have been popular in the 1930s, but after the end of World War Two and the fear of communism began to seep in, it was thought that the CSA was nothing more than a socialist or communist front. Some Congregationalists grew wary enough of the organization to create a counter group in 1952 called the Committee Opposing Congregational Political Action (COCPA). This group charged that the CSA was really nothing more than a "materialistic and immoral" organization, attempting to present itself as a Christian one.

The COPCA insisted that rugged individualism and not collective socialism was the true spirit of their Puritan forbearers and that the measures that the CSA called for were complete anathema to Congregationalist ideals. In this atmosphere, the Congregationalists began to go into decline. They ended up holding what would be one of their last main gatherings in the year 1956.

The following year, in 1957, the two factions of the Congregationalists—the Evangelical and Reformed Church and the General Council of the Congregational Christian Churches—actually merged together to become the United Church of Christ or, as it is otherwise simply known, the UCC. It was the UCC that, in great fanfare in November of 1970, celebrated the 350th anniversary of the Pilgrims' landing at Plymouth.

The UCC ran a piece in one of their publications, *The United Church Herald*, in which they praised the Pilgrims and their Puritan ways. The publication gushed over how these seekers of religious freedom had "practiced democracy, independence and congregationalism [even] before they had been defined." However, not all old-school Puritans were happy with the UCC, and its formation would lead to the establishment of the National Association of Congregational Christian Churches, which was essentially put together in protest of the UCC's founding. It was here that the hardliners of the old Puritan ideals sought to find a place for themselves. Those that were a part of the National Association of Congregational Christian Churches believed that they were the true heirs of both Puritan beliefs and spirit.

The UCC, in the meantime, became increasingly liberal in its views and found itself welcoming a wide range of religious thought, as well as accepting folks who hailed from a wide range of social backgrounds. For a church whose ancestors frowned upon something as simple as dancing and singing, the liberal amount of acceptance that the UCC congregants now espoused was quite a transformation. As the UCC continued its more liberal bent, they would give rise to controversial pastors, such as Reverend Jeremiah Wright.

Jeremiah Wright was the pastor of a United Church of Christ congregation in Chicago. He gained media scrutiny during the 2008 presidential election due to his connection to candidate Barack Obama, who used to attend Wright's church. During the presidential campaign, several old video clips of Wright's preaching began to surface in which Wright seemed to be making anti-Semitic and other controversial remarks. Obama quickly denounced Wright's words, and Wright himself went on the record to say that he "misspoke." Some clever pundits in the media recognized that Wright's church had Puritan roots and began to joke that perhaps his tirades were simply his version of the old Puritan "jeremiad."

The UCC church from which Jeremiah Wright hailed was called Trinity United Church of Christ, which was founded in 1961. It was actually the first predominantly African American UCC church. Reverend Wright saw the church through plenty of turbulent times, and by his own admission, he had developed a mindset of not holding anything back. He believed in speaking truth to power or at least his version of the truth.

As controversial as someone like Wright had become, he was from the tradition of Congregationalist churches, which itself was founded by the Puritans. Those folks who wanted to establish a shining city on a hill for the world to see probably had no idea that that one of the inheritors of their tradition would be a man who would be seen openly cursing America from the pulpit. So much for that shining city on a hill!

But then again, it would be wrong to say that Wright completely strayed from Puritan ideals. It was the Puritans, after all, who stressed the need for a pastor to be able to speak freely to his congregations without the oversight of regional authority figures. The fact that Wright was speaking his mind and independently attending to his flock is indeed in line with the general Puritan drive for freedom of worship and religious expression being unhindered within church walls.

The United Church of Christ is a liberal-leaning congregation, and its progressive nature, in many ways, does seem to be in stark contrast to the ultra-conservative roots of the Puritan movement. It is hard telling what some of the originators of the movement would think of these changes. The UCC has been criticized in recent years for focusing too much on social justice and being "too politically correct." In 2011, this so-called political correctness was on full display when the UCC decided to go gender-neutral in references to God. Instead of saying "Heavenly Father," for example, it was decided that God would be referred to as simply "Triune God." This move was somewhat backtracked since even some congregants of the UCC were uncomfortable with it. But if you really get down to it, it's perhaps a little perplexing that we envision God to have a gender at all. Even Jesus seemed to discount this notion when he seemed to remark on the genderless nature of heavenly beings. Angels, although described as having a male appearance in the Bible, are generally viewed to be genderless in the literal sense of the word. At one point in his ministry, Jesus was asked a rather witty question about who someone with multiple marriage partners would end up with in the afterlife. Jesus told them, "For when they shall rise from the dead, they neither marry, nor are given in marriage; but are as the angels which are in heaven." (Matthew 12:25)

The UCC comes from a long line of thought-provoking theologians such as Anne Hutchinson, Cotton Mather, and Jonathan Edwards. Having said that, it shouldn't be all that surprising that their descendants continue to push boundaries, even if it were something that their own forebearers may not have necessarily approved of.

Today, the UCC likes to set itself apart from its peers by proclaiming that it is a church in which the "Lord is still speaking." The founding fathers of the Puritan movement may not agree with all of the efforts taking place within the UCC, but they would have to agree with the general spirit behind it.

Chapter 11 – A Day in the Life of a Puritan

"Feelings come and feelings go, and feelings are deceiving; My warrant is the Word of God—Naught else is worth believing. Though all my heart should feel condemned for want of some sweet token. There is one greater than my heart whose word cannot be broken. I'll trust in God's unchanging word till should and body sever. For, though all things shall pass away, his word shall stand forever."

-Martin Luther

In the Puritan tradition of today, you may be surprised to find congregants having a wide range of viewpoints on key aspects of religious doctrine. This is in stark contrast to the way that the Puritans began their existence.

The Puritan belief system was centered around one's identification of God as the sole authority in one's life and the perfection of obedience to God. Puritans, as was evidenced during the Salem witch trials, truly believed that unseen forces were at work in their lives. They took to heart the words of the Apostle Paul, who stated that we "look through a glass darkly." They held firm that even those who clearly understood the scripture could not fully come to grips with the spiritual world since they themselves were still chained to the world of flesh and blood by virtue of merely being alive. As an Anglican peer of the Puritans once declared, it might be "possible to apprehend God"; however, it's not quite so easy "to comprehend God."

Nevertheless, the Puritans knew that some aspects of God could be understood simply by looking out at the world that He had designed and created. Just by pondering the cut-and-dried facts of creation, one can find evidence of a divine designer. The moon, for example, which is considerably smaller than the sun, just so happens to be, at times, positioned in just the right place in space to appear to cover the sun's solar face, rendering a solar eclipse for those of us down here on Earth. It's certainly a rather convenient coincidence, isn't it? People around the world have enjoyed total solar eclipses since the dawn of time, with most completely unaware of how unlikely such an event actually is. Many scientists have also agreed that the odds of this occurring at random are too incredible to fathom. The sun is over 93 million miles from Earth, and it has a diameter of about 864,948 miles. The moon, on the other hand, is much closer at just 238,900 miles away, and it has a diameter of just 2,158 miles. In other words, the sun is really big, while the moon is much smaller in comparison. Yet, somehow or other, when we look up at the sky, from our vantage point, we get to see two celestial objects that appear roughly the same size, and when they cross paths, they have the potential of creating a total eclipse. It would seem that these two completely different objects were put in place just for us to admire it all. Or as King David of the Bible once wrote in one of his many Psalms, "The heavens declare the glory of God; the skies proclaim the work of his hands" (Psalm 19:1).

This is indeed one of the signs a Puritan would have pointed to as it pertains to the obviously intelligent design of the universe. But as it pertained to the spiritual nature of the universe, which could not be fathomed, the Puritans turned to the Bible for answers. If, for example, someone suddenly became ill and rapidly perished, it wouldn't be unusual for a Puritan to ascribe some divine meaning behind it. Was there a reason that this person perished like this? What was God trying to tell us?

They also applied such questioning to themselves collectively as a whole. This was done with the infamous jeremiads, in which, like the prophet Jeremiah, current hardships were interpreted as being a judgment from God and a warning for the flock to turn "from their wicked ways."

Interestingly enough, however, as it pertained to the Puritans, as much as they sought to set themselves apart with their own brand of puritanical beliefs, they too suffered from eventual divisions, schisms, and theological splits. The truth is there never really was one single unified Puritan approach to religion other than the notion of striving to set themselves apart from the religious mainstream of the time, which they collectively disdained. It is precisely this lack of unified doctrine that leads most scholars to point to Puritanism as being more akin to a movement rather than a static denomination of Christian religion.

One of the fascinating aspects of puritanical beliefs was that although they held firm to the doctrine of predestination, they still stressed living as faithfully as possible. The idea that whoever goes to heaven or hell has already been predetermined might make one tempted to slack off a bit, as no amount of good works would ever change that fact. But not the Puritans! Even though they believed that it was all predetermined, they were sure to do their best, to be the shining city on a hill that John Winthrop so fondly spoke of. Despite their belief in predestination, the Puritans did everything they could to live what they believed to be a godly life.

One might wonder if Puritans believed that it was all preordained, why were they trying so hard to live out their own personal version of what constitutes a pure life? The Puritans believed that they were supposed to be examples to others, and they saw themselves as fulfilling God's will by the lives that they lived. Whether it was preordained or not, the Puritans were more than ready to play the part. Puritans also wanted to reassure themselves that they were indeed preordained for salvation.

It might sound a little convoluted, but they felt that since the fruits of their works bore witness to their overall state of being, they wanted to make sure that their fruit was good. This was a witness not only to their neighbors but also to themselves of God's goodness and, by extension, this goodness at work in their own lives. If they were doing good and generally enjoyed doing good, then they could rest assured that it must have been preordained by God that they would be saved.

Despite the stereotype of Puritans being a bunch of dour-faced people who hated to have a good time, the Puritans actually had a healthy sense of fun. They weren't all work and no play; they just insisted that their joyful activities be highly regimented. They felt that there was a time and place for everything, and they believed that their lives should follow a specific organizational structure. While it was okay to have time at the end of the day to joke around with your family in the house, it would have been viewed as highly inappropriate to be cutting up like this in the middle of a church sermon. It wasn't that the act of goofing off was really that bad; it was more that it would be inappropriate in a church setting.

For the Puritan Pilgrims, their greatest sense of enjoyment came from their time spent with nature. For a Puritan back then, a typical Sunday would have involved church service in the morning and then an afternoon spent communing with nature. Picnics would have been in order, and fishing and berry picking in the surrounding area would have been quite common.

But even in these endeavors, it was viewed that they should only be done if they served a general purpose. Fishing and then wasting the fish you just caught, for example, would have been frowned upon. So whatever fish were kept undoubtedly would have ended up on the fire later that night for dinner.

The needless bloodshed of an animal was always considered wrong, which was evidenced by the fact that the Puritans banned cockfighting. Most today would agree with the Puritans that cockfighting, which entails a crowd of people watching two birds peck each other to death, is rather cruel. But at the time, the Puritans were more the exception than the rule, as other colonists wouldn't have thought much of it. The idea of watching animals fight each other for entertainment is wrong on many levels, and the Puritans preached as much, letting it be known that there would be no room for anyone of the Puritan faith to include any so-called "blood sports" in their recreational lives.

It was for this same reason that the Puritans would refuse to take part in a game like football, which, especially in its more primitive era, would indeed have been labeled a blood sport. Another pastime that the Puritans frowned upon was the enjoyment of theatrical productions. When Oliver Cromwell came to power in the 1650s, under heavy Puritan influence (the heaviest England would ever have), he put a stop to the popular production of plays outright. This was a temporary setback for theater lovers and thespians in England, but the Puritans of the New England colonies maintained this rigid ban of the theater for several more decades to come.

When it came to the pastime of music, Puritans were a little more ambivalent. While they disliked the traditional chorus and instrumental-based music that the Church of England had inherited from the Catholic Church, they encouraged the singing of psalms, and within Puritan households, the playing of musical instruments was eventually quite common.

One of the most treasured pastimes of the Puritans, as was experienced by the first Thanksgiving, was feasting. Basically, this was the idea of setting aside a day to bring a bunch of food and have communal fellowship with friends, family, and neighbors. It was at these great feasts that Puritans shared the latest developments, joked around, and generally enjoyed the company of one another.

This was always the greatest strength of the Congregationalists—their strong sense of community. Even before they stepped foot on land, their Pilgrim forebearers were sure to forge a tight social compact, right there in the quarters of their ship. With this, they were armed with a tight social protocol of how they would deal with not just themselves but also anyone else whom they might encounter.

The Puritan gift of good food and open dialogue proved itself to be highly successful when it came to negotiations with the local Native American population already living in New England. The fact that the first few decades of the Puritan settlement were virtually unmarred by any violence between these two very different peoples is a testament to this strong social compact at work.

The Puritans, you see, were pioneers in every sense of the word. Yes, they were literal trailblazers who burned a path through the wilderness, but they were also pioneers in the sense of just how far-reaching their diplomatic relations were. They were ready and willing to meet others halfway. When dealing with a native delegation, for example, it wouldn't be uncommon for a group of Puritans to travel all the way into the middle of a wooded area that was patrolled by roving bands of tribal warriors. The Puritans were indeed bold, and this boldness was no doubt a boldness inspired by their strong belief in God.

Many Puritans felt they were on a divine mission of providence. They furthermore believed that God had preordained their ultimate success. This was their true wellspring of courage. The Puritans figured that God was on their side, and with the creator of the very universe looking after you like that, what's there to fear? This was indeed the general mindset that most New England Puritans tended to have. And the sheer audacity and courage they put on display every day of their lives bore testament to that fact.

Conclusion: They Let Their Light Shine

Although the Puritans were a powerful movement and a direct result of the Protestant Reformation, most today likely don't know a whole lot about them. Perhaps they make the connection that the Pilgrims from the *Mayflower* who dressed funny and ate turkey on Thanksgiving had something to do with them, but it usually doesn't go too much further than that. Then again, some might consider the Salem witch trials and realize the Puritan connection there.

Either way, both of these associations paint the Puritans in larger-than-life and entirely stereotypical portraits that do not quite reflect reality. The Puritans were indeed on the *Mayflower*, and they did host a series of witch trials in Salem, but this doesn't tell anyone the full story of the group. In order to best understand the Puritans, one first has to consider what drove them to set themselves apart in the first place. It was their deep ideological longing for something greater than the typical religious trappings they had experienced.

The Church of England, from whence the Puritans had originally sprung, proved itself to be far too stifling and retroactive of a vehicle for English Protestants who wished to truly reform the way that their religious services were carried out. Even though the British had broken with the Catholic Church, in many ways, it seemed that England was merely Protestant in name only since so many trappings of the Catholic Church remained in place. It was these last vestiges of Catholicism that the Puritans sought to purge. They wished not so much to create a new religion or denomination as much as they simply wanted to purify the brand of faith that they already had. By the time of Oliver Cromwell, the Puritan-friendly Lord Protector of England, many Puritan-minded believers felt that they had finally been given their chance to truly transform their religion.

But when Cromwell perished, much of this hope died with him. England then went through a series of rulers who, at times, were somewhat open to reform but also routinely backtracked on measures that were viewed as being of the utmost importance to the Protestant faithful. It was when the situation was no longer tolerable in England that many Puritans began to look toward the Americas as a permanent refuge for their flock.

The Pilgrims of the *Mayflower* in 1620, followed by John Winthrop's major wave of Puritans in 1630, proved that the Puritans could not only survive in the New World but also—just as Winthrop had described it—set themselves up as a "city on a hill." They believed that even if the situation may have been unfavorable in Britain, if they could just provide a good enough example in the American colonies, they might be able to change the minds of those who had previously opposed them. All they had to do was let their light shine.

Here's another book by Captivating History that you might like

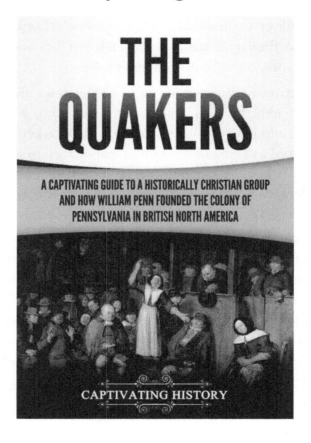

Free Bonus from Captivating History (Available for a Limited time)

Hi History Lovers!

Now you have a chance to join our exclusive history list so you can get your first history ebook for free as well as discounts and a potential to get more history books for free! Simply visit the link below to join.

Captivatinghistory.com/ebook

Also, make sure to follow us on Facebook, Twitter and Youtube by searching for Captivating History.

Appendix A: Further Reading and Reference

Killing England: The Brutal Struggle for American Independence. Bill O'Reilly, 2017.

As a City on a Hill: The Story of America's Most Famous Lay Sermon. Daniel T. Rodgers, 2018.

The Puritan Experiment: New England Society from Bradford to Edwards. Francis J. Bremer, 1976.

The Last Puritans: Mainline Protestants and the Power of the Past. Margaret Bendroth, 2015.

The Puritans: A Transatlantic History. David D. Hall, 2019.

Pilgrims and Puritans: 1620-1676. Christopher Collier & James Lincoln Collier, 1998.

Who Were the Accused Witches of Salem? And Other Questions about the Witchcraft Trials. Laura Hamilton Waxman, 2012.

Reformation: A World in Turmoil. Andrew Atherstone, 2015.

A Delusion of Satan: The Full Story of the Salem Witch Trials. Frances Hill, 2002.

Made in United States
Orlando, FL
01 July 2023

34682212R00055